MAKE
IT

How to deliver high-stakes
presentations to people you
need to impress at work

COUNT

Alex Merry

WWW.GET-KNOWN.CO.UK

To Livvy, Mum, Dad, William and Emily.
Oh and to our dog Margot, who will no doubt chew
any of the copies I keep at home.

CONTENTS

INTRODUCTION ...9

PART 1: CLARITY ...29

PART 2: CONNECTION ...79

PART 3: CONFIDENCE ...133

CONCLUSION ...183

INTRODUCTION

THE PRESENTATION HABITS THAT FRUSTRATE LEADERS THE MOST

In preparation for writing this book I asked myself a question. 'Who are the most intimidatingly impressive leaders that I know?'

Over the last few years I've been lucky enough to meet (and present to) quite a few. Either by chance, curating the speaker line-up at TEDxClapham, or because they've been clients.

The litmus test was simple. If the thought of presenting to them made me nervous, they made the cut!

Then I reached out and asked three questions:

1. What are the presentation habits that frustrate you the most?

2. What are the most common traits of a presentation that misses the mark?

3.   Imagine a member of the team has just delivered the
      perfect presentation. What was so good about it?

And I made it clear to them that the type of presentations
I was interested in were not the inspiring TED talks or the
motivational commencement speeches, but the presentations that happen behind the scenes. The ones that you can't
just look up online and try to emulate. The ones that nobody
teaches us how to do effectively. The ones that get things
done and make things happen inside organisations.

      Twenty people responded. A mixture of founders and
CEOs of businesses with nine-figure valuations, CXOs of
global brands, investors, VCs, a former brigadier from the
British Army and even one of Britain's top politicians.

      Some of the answers were expected. For example, the
most common pet hates included:

'Starting a presentation with an apology.'

'Reading from the slides.'

'Going into too much detail.'

'A lack of interaction.'

'Overformality and nervousness.'

Others were more surprising. Things like:

'What do you want from us?! Are you trying to get a decision? Need input on a problem? Just sharing info? Tell us!'

'Don't just dive straight in – we might be time-poor, but context is critical.'

'Stop trying to prove to us you've done a lot of work. Instead, share insights that reveal things we never knew about our business.'

Their answers have been distilled into three key themes that have gone on to both validate and shape the content of this book.

Part 1 is about clarity. In it, you will be given the six-part structure to create an impactful presentation. You'll learn how to distil complex messages in a single sentence and take your audience on a journey that creates buy-in. Come the end of this section, you'll have everything you need to create presentations that your audience will remember and that you will be proud to deliver. When you know that what you've got to say is good, you'll carry that self-belief into the presentations with you.

Part 2 is about connection. It's packed full of tricks about how to engage an audience, both in person and online. You'll learn how to speak with more gravitas and use your body language to change the energy in a room. Then you'll be ready for my tried-and-tested slide deck, designed to save you a load of time and your audience from information overload. By the end of this section, you'll be able to impress the most demanding audiences with your presentation skills.

Part 3 is about confidence. By the time you get to this part of the book, you'll already have more confidence in what you're going to say and how you're going to say it. But this section isn't about that. It's about the confidence that you and your audience can't see. You're going to learn how to quieten the mind, overcome self-doubt and prevent nerves from getting the better of you in high-stake presentation scenarios.

I designed this book for people like me. People who aren't natural performers, who don't seek the limelight, yet find themselves in professional situations where they're expected to present at a high level.

This process is not about becoming a big-stage conference speaker, it's about bringing high-stakes presentations into your comfort zone at work.

Let's get to work!

WHO THIS BOOK IS AND ISN'T FOR

This book is for anyone who has to deliver presentations internally at work to people they need to impress. Management, senior leadership, the board, your investors, your boss – whoever it is, the stakes are high and you need to make it count.

You may have to present quarterly updates, seek approval for ideas or pitch for budget, and the chances are it's something that you endure rather than enjoy.

- Do you feel ill-equipped to communicate at the level that's expected of you?

- Are you fed up of the pre-presentation dread and over-preparation?

- Does every presentation feel like a test?

- Get the impression you drown your audience in detail?

- Done with presentations draining your energy?

There comes a time in your career where the presentations you're being asked to deliver are too important to just get through. You need to nail them.

The very fact you find yourself in this situation tells me that some important people think that what you've got to say is worth listening to. Like it or not, this means that your presentations have potential, which is a perfect starting point.

You're not here to become a TEDx speaker or get standing ovations at industry conferences. You're here to deliver presentations that land at work, consistently and comfortably. Without overwhelming your audience and without the current levels of physical, mental and emotional disruption to your life that come from feeling like you're presenting to a jury.

Challenge accepted.

HOW TO USE THIS BOOK

There's a reason why this book is so short. It's designed to be used, not just read.

To get the most out of it, my suggestion would be to read it from cover to cover first. It'll only take you about 90 minutes and you'll already be a better and happier presenter for it. After that, treat it like your very own presentation coach. Check in with the section you need, when you need it.

Part 1 is your content coach. When you've got a presentation coming up, it is there to ask you all the right questions to ensure your message is clear and your presentation lands.

Part 2 is your presence coach. Its goal is to make you as engaging as possible so you own the room you're presenting in.

Part 3 is your mindset coach. Every time you're experiencing nerves, self-doubt or pre-presentation anxiety, it will be there to help you perform at your best when it matters.

These three sections will give you a solid foundation for supercharging your presenting skills, but to go even further you're going to need my Presenter's Toolkit.

In it, you'll get all the frameworks and resources mentioned in the book, including:

- three failsafe ways to open your next presentation

- eight powerful stories to incorporate into your next presentation

- four ways to close a presentation with impact

- the Speedy Speech-Writing Framework, designed to save you hours of needless presentation creation

- a beautifully crafted slide deck template that will help make sure your own decks don't distract or overwhelm your audience

- a data storytelling masterclass that will help you bring your data to life.

You'll also get special access to MicDrop Analytics, my presentation analysis platform, and a playlist specially designed to calm the mind and get you into the zone.

Get access now and then you'll be able to follow along when Toolkit items are referenced in the book. Just scan the QR code below or head to:

https://alexmerry.com/mic-presenters-toolkit.

WHY DOES GIVING A PRESENTATION FEEL LIKE SUCH A BURDEN?

Meet Clara. A successful thirty-something who was promoted to a senior role at a high-profile organisation a few months back. Around the office, she is well-liked and respected by her colleagues, and if you were to bump into her at work, it wouldn't take you long to work out why: she is personable, hardworking, and intelligent. She is someone who has enjoyed her work and has always taken pride in the fact that she is seen as the reliable one. The go-to person for the most important jobs. But ever since she landed her new position, things haven't quite been the same.

One of the expectations of her new role is that she's got to deliver formal presentations to people who she feels are both intimidatingly impressive and far better qualified to talk about her subject than she is. The first time she had to present to senior leadership she put in hours of overtime preparing her content and her slide deck, desperate to make a good first impression and validate the reason why she had been given the position in the first place.

Yet all that effort resulted in her being pulled in by her manager for some 'feedback' and being told that she needs to 'improve her executive presence' because 'her message wasn't landing'. Those words hit her like a truck and expelled any of the 'fake it till you make it' faux-confidence that she had left. That was the moment her 'reliable one' image shattered and it has cast a shadow of doubt on her work life ever since. For the first time in her career, she feels ashamed and unsure; not that she'd admit it.

On the days she has to go into the office, her commute is spent hoping that she doesn't bump into and have to make awkward conversation with one of the other senior leaders who also makes a point of turning up earlier than everyone else. The commute is her last few minutes of calm, normally spent psyching herself up for the day ahead. As she walks through the entrance of the office she takes a deep breath, exhales a sigh and turns on 'professional Clara'. The version of herself she has adopted to ease the transition into leadership.

In her first meeting of the day, one of the other newly promoted members of the team has been asked to present a product roadmap, and seems to be completely at ease. The manager who gave her that confidence-destroying feedback the other day is in the room too. She looks around, and the audience seems super engaged. It's as though everything that is coming out of the presenter's mouth is gold dust. So rather than listening to what is actually being said, Clara decides the time would be better spent analysing everything that the presenter is doing. Maybe I could copy them, she thinks. But she realises that to do so would mean she'd have to become someone she's not, and the one thing she does know about effective presenting is you have to be authentic.

They're making it look effortless, but they don't seem to be doing anything that special, she thinks. As time goes on, she secretly hopes for something to go wrong. Nothing major, perhaps just a question from someone that shows they don't have all the answers, a crack in this seemingly flawless performance. It doesn't come. When the floor opens for questions, although she has something to say, she ends up talking herself out of sharing it. At the end of the meeting, she notices her manager go over and thank the presenter for a good job well done and an insightful presentation well delivered.

She returns to her desk, questioning what exactly she needs to do to make the leap to present so effortlessly, and feeling frustrated that she doesn't have the answer.

She thinks, I'm good at what I do, yet when I have to talk about it, I'm my own worst enemy. How do I stop getting in the way of myself? And why can't I present as effortlessly as everyone else seems to be able to?

Trying to wrap her head around this paradox only compounds her issues. It just doesn't make sense. She thinks back to the good old days when she could avoid delivering presentations because there were others in the team who were happy to do it.

She goes out for a walk at lunch. It's an opportunity to reset and put an end to her morning of judgement and comparison. When she gets back to her desk, she returns to an email titled 'Quick one…'. It's from her manager.

'Do you mind delivering an update to the board next week?' Written in a tone so trivial she might as well have been asked whether she'd had a good weekend.

'Well actually, yes I do,' is what she wants to write, but instead, she replies 'No problem,' trying to make the response seem as casual as the email she'd just received. The moment she presses send, the countdown begins.

The first thing she does is check her calendar. After the amount of time she'd spent prepping that last disaster of a presentation, she knows she needs to put in even more time now – which according to her diary is a scarce commodity. To top it off, she's due to be meeting some friends the night before the presentation, and without thinking she drops them a message to cancel. I've probably done them a favour, she thinks. I'm hardly going to be the life and soul of the party that evening. Instead, I'll use that time to do my final preparation and get an early (and sleepless) night instead, so I'm at least giving myself the best chance of doing myself justice on the day.

On the way out of the office, she bumps into the person that presented at the meeting this morning. She considers asking them for some advice but thinks better of it. This is something I've got to tackle alone…

Now, Clara might think she's the only one at her level who hasn't got public speaking nailed, but in fact, the opposite is true. As your career progresses you are increasingly likely to find yourself in situations where you are expected to present in front of important people. As a result, it's very natural to feel like you're out of your depth, to the point where it's overshadowing all the things that have resulted in you being the one asked to speak about them in the first place. What also doesn't help is when management step in and offer feedback that might be well-meaning but almost always results in the recipient falling down a spiral of self-doubt, compounding the anxiety next time round.

'You don't sound as confident as you think you do.'

'You need to present with more authority.'

'These are really important people with no time to waste, don't overcomplicate it, just get to the point!'

Almost everyone will receive this 'feedback' at some point in their career. Not that you'll hear about it. One of the strange, unwritten rules of the world of work seems to be that the more responsibility you are given (sorry, I mean 'empowered' with), the less help you need, so asking for help feels like a sign of weakness and one that you can't afford to show.

You're not alone, and there's certainly nothing wrong with you. But the bottom line is this…

Although you're great at what you do, whatever got you to where you are now will not carry you through. You need to learn the next level of how to play the game.

The second thing to note here is that there is a cost to reacting in the way that Clara did. It takes up far too much of your energy, to the point where it is impacting your ability to lead. And if you fall into the trap, like so many others do, of just accepting that this is the way it is, eventually this gap in your confidence will grow and seep into other areas of your life.

I know you want to do a good job. I know you're worried and I get that, but when a looming presentation is such a source of stress and worry, it's not just a shame, it's a waste. You're making life hard on yourself and you're applying the brakes on your career because deep down, you'll always be waiting for the next presentation to land in your inbox.

The good news is that it doesn't have to be this way. Delivering high-stakes presentations that impress the people around you doesn't need to be exhausting, and the best news is that it's a skill you can learn. One that will free up your energy, open up a whole world of opportunities for your career and create more fulfilment at work. And that is incredibly exciting.

Three experiences that have shaped my philosophy as a public speaking coach

---

WHO AM I?

When people first find out I'm a public speaking coach, they tend to make two assumptions. One is that I love presenting, and the other is that I come from some sort of performance background.

Neither of which is true.

I don't like public speaking. In fact, I've spent the majority of my life avoiding it like the plague. To this day, I don't wake up in the morning feeling excited that I'm delivering a presentation later on. But what does excite me is what happens when you get them right. They magnify your ability to effect change. They are a force multiplier for all the other skills that you bring to the table and they are an opportunity to challenge yourself.

I don't come from a performance background either. Before I became a public speaking coach, I spent seven years as the COO of a London start-up. I accepted the job straight out of university, blissfully ignorant that delivering presentations would become our growth strategy. I had to become a good presenter because, like you, I didn't have a choice.

I'm writing this book because I want to unlock what being able to deliver presentations well can do for you.

If you'd like to say hello:

alex@alexmerry.com

www.linkedin.com/in/mralexmerry/

LESSON 1: EVEN THE MOST COMPETENT PRESENTERS HAVE THEIR BAD DAYS

When I was working at the London start-up, Alasdair the CEO and I would spend three months each year living out of a Peugeot 307 on a recruitment tour. We'd visit the UK's top universities to deliver a 1-hour presentation with the aim of convincing students to spend their summers fund-raising for charity door to door. This was long before businesses were using social media, which meant that when we arrived each morning, nobody knew who on earth we were.

So Alasdair invented the 'lecture shout'. This involved finding the biggest lecture theatres on campus and delivering a 60-second elevator pitch designed to persuade 300+ students to turn up to a lunchtime information meeting where they'd find out about a summer job opportunity.

At the end of the pitch, we would hold up these flyers (which we called 'tickets' to elevate their value) and say: 'So for those of you who are interested in finding out more, we're holding a meeting today at 1pm and you're going to need one of these tickets to get in. If you'd like a ticket, put your hand up now and I'll make sure you get one.'

And then we'd wait, trying to hold our nerve, praying that at least someone volunteered their hand. Sometimes these pitches went well and there would be a Mexican wave of hands go up (and a huge sigh of relief), and other times there'd be deadpan silence, at which point we would begin the walk of shame out of the lecture hall and spend the next hour psyching ourselves up for the next lecture.

By the time the information meeting came around, we'd have presented to the best part of 1,000 students and then the real work began. Students aren't afraid to say what they really think. If a meeting wasn't going well, we'd be on the receiving end of heckles and people walking out 10 minutes in when they realised the job involved door to door sales.

We did this five days a week, for three months a year, for seven years.

As a presentation bootcamp, it was as brutal as it was transformational. However, there are far easier ways to bring presenting into your comfort zone.

What's interesting is that even with years of experience under my belt, I still had days where things didn't go to plan. Lecture shouts that resulted in the walk of shame and information meetings where the audience morphed into a mob.

This book isn't going to stop you from having the odd shocker, but it will help you to improve the way you deal with them. One disappointing performance shouldn't shatter your confidence.

LESSON 2: ONE GOOD PRESENTATION CAN CREATE UNTHINKABLE OPPORTUNITIES

The day after one of those recruitment meetings, my PA forwarded on an email from someone who'd attended, asking me to speak at their event. I checked out the website and it was an event run by some organisation called TEDx. Never heard of it, but it looked impressive. Sure. Why not?! (Clearly, public speaking was very much in my comfort zone by this point.)

Much to my frustration back then and my relief now (because the talk I was planning would not have been good for my brand!), the event was cancelled at the last minute. So I spent the next two years trying to convince TEDx to let me run my own event.

When they did, I set up TEDxClapham as a side project. Little did I know at the time, this was the start of my public speaking coaching journey.

In the lead up to each event, I used my own experience to help the speakers prepare for the stage. Most speakers would fall into two camps. Those who had no clear message but were highly engaging, and those who had a powerful message that wasn't landing because their nerves were getting in the way. My job was to ensure that by the time each speaker stepped on stage, they had both.

Some of those talks inspired others to lobby the UN and change government legislation. Others went viral, creating multi-million-pound opportunities and resulting in book deals.

With the right process in place, presentations can bring disproportionate value to you and the people you're speaking to.

LESSON 3: SOME OF THE BEST PEOPLE GO UNNOTICED

When I was curating TEDxClapham, it always seemed to be the most reluctant presenters whose talks ended up having the most impact. It made me realise that the opportunities are often only given to those who have the confidence to speak up and put themselves out there. While those who don't get overlooked. If it's a problem in the world of thought leadership, it must be a drop in the ocean compared to the world of work. A place where the opportunities go to those who have the confidence to put themselves out there and impress the right people. The 'confident' ones, by the way, are a minority and they aren't necessarily the ones that have the most valuable and interesting things to say.

The world is missing out on so much value from those who keep quiet because they second-guess themselves or don't believe that what they've got to say is worth listening to.

My focus has been on solving this problem ever since and I've seen first hand what an absolute gamechanger bringing high-pressure presentations into your comfort zone is for your career and your fulfilment at work. Not only do they help you get noticed, but those who possess the skill seem to bring an inner confidence to everything else they do. In this book, I'm going to share with you the techniques that I teach at fast-growing scale-ups like Bumble and WeTransfer to corporate juggernauts like Bloomberg and Amazon.

PART 1

———

CLARITY

What you
say matters

———

My reputation as a public speaking coach has been built on one simple principle born out of the frustration of sitting through too many presentations that have missed the mark, both as a COO and when curating the line-up for TEDxClapham.

What you say matters.

I'm not alone in thinking this. Comments from the senior leaders I interviewed included:

> 'Providing tons of info is no use to me at all. I've got enough on my plate. Get to the "so what" quicker!'

> 'What I'm looking for are useful insights. What I all too often get is the presenter trying to prove that they've done a lot of work.'

'I find people often haven't thought about the key takea-way when creating a presentation.'

I empathise with them. But I also empathise with you.

How are you supposed to know what you need to share, how much detail your audience wants, and how to package it memorably when you're speaking to a group that a) you may have never met before and b) has expertise in a completely different part of the business?!

Working out the 'what' is difficult, but it's important and it's something we'll look at how to do later on. In fact, the 'what' is the reason you have been asked to deliver a presentation in the first place. You have information and insights that are valuable to leadership. When you know how to articulate them with clarity, your presentations will become a welcome breath of fresh air for the senior leaders in your audience.

The three types of presentation purpose

---

1. GET CLEAR ON THE BRIEF

Most presentations are doomed to fail because they are requested like this: 'Please can you prepare a 15-minute update for next month's senior management meeting?'

It's an excruciatingly vague request.

The word 'update' suggests that they want to know how things are going. If that was all they really wanted, they'd have asked you to send it in an email.

The problem is the people you're presenting to don't know how to articulate what they want, so they use the word 'update' to compensate and expect you to just know what they mean. What they are really after are insights: information that improves their understanding of the projects you're working on.

A better ask might be to 'share learnings that will help us make better decisions moving forward'. Not as succinct, but certainly more helpful.

But before we blame the messenger, remember that they can't act as a mind-reader and provide you with exactly what you want every time. Sometimes it's down to you to get that information out of them.

So the next time you're on the receiving end of such a vague request, instead of replying 'no problem' and proceeding to make assumptions about what is and isn't relevant, you'd be far better off replying with an email that looks something like this:

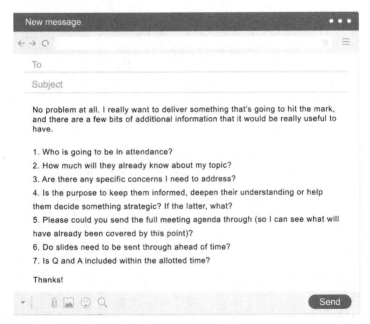

New message

To

Subject

No problem at all. I really want to deliver something that's going to hit the mark, and there are a few bits of additional information that it would be really useful to have.

1. Who is going to be in attendance?
2. How much will they already know about my topic?
3. Are there any specific concerns I need to address?
4. Is the purpose to keep them informed, deepen their understanding or help them decide something strategic? If the latter, what?
5. Please could you send the full meeting agenda through (so I can see what will have already been covered by this point)?
6. Do slides need to be sent through ahead of time?
7. Is Q and A included within the allotted time?

Thanks!

Send

If the thought of sending an email like this feels as if you're burdening the person who asked you to present, or will reflect badly on you because you feel like you're expected to just know these things, here is something to consider: if you're delivering a 15-minute presentation to 10 people, you are responsible for 150 minutes or 2.5 hours of time. The 10 minutes it will take someone to answer the above questions to ensure that time isn't wasted is something that both the messenger and your audience will thank you for.

2. ESTABLISH A PURPOSE

There are two factors that need to be taken into account when it comes to deciding on your presentation's purpose.

The first is the needs of your audience, and the answers to the questions in the sample email above will give you the clarity you need from their perspective.

The second (which is all too often overlooked) is your own needs. Gone are the days when presenting is a one-way exchange. The reason you're being asked to present in the first place is because of the unique perspective that you have on the business. This is why it is so important you take the time to consider what you need to get from the presentation so you're able to do your job better. That way everyone in the room wins.

Most presentations fall into one of three purpose categories:

To update

This is an opportunity to manage up by increasing transparency and raising awareness.

The goal is to manage your audience's expectations, by making it clear how things are really progressing.

Their gift is peace of mind if things are going well, and if times are tough, at least forewarned is forearmed.

To educate

This is an opportunity to position yourself as a subject-matter expert.

The goal is to widen the scope of your audience's knowledge so they are able to make better decisions faster.

Their gift is the confidence they have in those decisions… decisions which you're likely to be on the receiving end of.

To persuade

This is an opportunity to create buy-in or change opinions or behaviour.

The goal is to leave your audience in no doubt of the case you are making.

Their gift is the satisfaction of progress, coming in the form of relief that a nagging problem can finally be solved, or excitement for what is to come.

A simple way to start clarifying your presentation's purpose is to consider your audience's pre-presentation and post-presentation attitudes, beliefs and knowledge.

In other words:

What do they think right now?

What do they need to think after my presentation?

This will help you determine where your presentation needs to take your audience from and to.

In the Toolkit (see page 13 if you haven't got access to it already), check out Tool 1 where I deep dive into how to determine your audience's pre- and post-presentation beliefs.

The gap between where your audience is and where you want them to be will uncover a problem that needs addressing and a message that needs sharing. Your audience may or may not be aware of this feeding into the presentation, and that's ok. But when you've identified exactly what that problem is, deciding on your presentation's purpose will become clearer.

Things aren't going to plan? A huge disparity between what leadership thinks is going on versus what's actually going on? Stuck and need some input? **It's time to update.**

Decisions from above hindering rather than helping progress? Leadership lacking expertise? Analysis paralysis preventing objectives from being achieved? **It's time to educate.**

Seeking approval for an idea? Pitching for more budget? Pushing for a change of direction? **It's time to persuade.**

In most cases, you will be choosing between updating and persuading. The presentations where educating is your sole focus will normally be easy to identify from the answers you get in your clarifying email.

When you have clarity of purpose, you're ready to start thinking about clarity of message.

3. DISTIL YOUR MESSAGE INTO A SINGLE SENTENCE

One of my favourite quotes is from the former chief design officer at Apple, Sir Jony Ive. He said, 'simplicity is the ultimate sophistication'. I think about that quote a lot. Looking back at the presentations that have had the biggest impact on me, the one thing they all have in common is that they can be distilled down to a single sentence. Ask anyone listening what the takeaway of the presentation is, and they'd all say the same thing.

One of the questions I would always ask in the TEDx-Clapham speaker application form is 'what is the core idea of your talk?' It was designed to test whether or not someone could communicate what they wanted to share in simple terms.

What I was hoping for was a one-sentence answer, but most of the answers I got back were overly complex and convoluted. For example:

> *'Women need to start businesses that make more money*
> *with less investment and hire self-perpetuating diverse*
> *teams who are better at innovation.'*

Contrast that with the answer I got back from the first speaker I ever invited to stand on that famous red spot:

> *'We need to change the definition of sexual assault.'*

A short, simple sentence that gives the audience absolute clarity in the message that's being shared. The speaker who delivered this talk was Isabel Oakley Chapman and, at the time, she was a couple of years out of university working in sex and relationship education.

There were plenty of far more qualified and experienced people that could have been standing on that stage instead of her, but it was her clarity of message that got her noticed.

We then spent the next few months working together on the content of her talk to make sure that this message was going to land with her audience (and come the end of the Clarity section of this book, you'll know exactly how you can do the same).

A few months later, she delivered the talk on the TEDxClapham stage. Two years later, I'm standing on a platform at Clapham Junction station and get a call...

'We did it!'

'Errr... hi Isabel... what exactly did we do?'

'The government have announced that they're changing the legislation to make sex and relationship education compulsory in English schools. My TEDx talk played a part in making that happen!'

'?!!!!!'

That presentation has catapulted her career. She now runs multiple organisations and community initiatives and was awarded an MBE by the Queen.

I'll always remember that phone call, and while I was shocked at the time, these days I am constantly being reminded of the power that one clear message and one well-crafted presentation can have, not just on thought leadership stages but in the world of work.

A great presentation starts with a memorable message.

The belief that the message will become clear after you've created the rest of the content is misguided, because without an anchor to centre your talk around, you're susceptible to going off on all sorts of tangents. This, in turn, will dilute your presentation's purpose and make it far harder for your message to be remembered.

It is for this reason that distilling your presentation's message into a single sentence before digging into the detail of your topic is time well spent.

Step 1: Use the formula

You can break any message down into three components:

- The **problem** – will have been pinpointed when choosing the presentation's purpose.

- The **solution** – your proposed means of overcoming the problem.

- The **impact** – what can be accomplished when that problem has been solved.

To create an effective message, you'll need to use two of the three components.
For example:

> *'Customer retention (problem) must become our number-one priority (solution).'*

> *'Inclusive language (solution) will help our company culture to flourish (impact).'*

> *'Software X (problem) is restricting our
> ability to scale (impact).'*

Step 2: Put it through the acid test

Next, use two of those three components to answer the following question.

What is the message I need my audience to remember?

The test for whether your sentence is strong enough is to insert 'The point is that…' in front of it. For example:

> *'The point is that customer retention must become our
> number-one priority.'*

If you need to adjust your sentence to make it fit, then do – it's an indicator your sentence still needs work. With a bit of wordplay you should have an insightful message that is:

- ✓ easy to understand, without needing context

- ✓ authoritative, with no words expressing uncertainty

- ✓ short – under 10 words long.

How to structure a presentation for impact

The most engaging, persuasive and impactful presentations all follow the same structure. When you know it, you'll be able to use it every time you're asked to present and it will save you a load of time and stress. But more importantly than that, when you know that what you've got to say is good, your confidence will increase and you'll deliver the presentation with more conviction as a result.

I know this because I've seen the impact it's had on clients who are still using this structure years after we've worked together. Just last week, this message landed in my inbox, from a client who heads up DEI in Europe for a company that has over 100,000 employees:

> *'That framework saved me yesterday when I was in a big panic! I used it for a meeting I had – it went well!'*

They were referring to my Speedy Speech-Writing Framework, which breaks every presentation down into 6 parts.

1. THE OPENER: GRAB THEIR ATTENTION

What not to do

We often make the assumption that because the people we're speaking to are time-poor, they want you to get straight to the point. But the truth is, no one is ready to hear the most important points of your presentation straight away. It takes time to tune out of whatever was happening before and then tune in to you and your topic, and the opener is about helping your audience do just that.

That said, most opening sections are often awkward, too slow and far too predictable. So predictable, in fact, that I've given the most common ones a name. Perhaps you might recognise some of these…

1. **The Awkward Apology**. 'Sorry, it's not the most exciting topic/I didn't have much time to prepare this/I'm not very good at presenting.'

    What's wrong? The most effective way to devalue everything you're about to say and frustrate the people you're speaking to. All the hard work you've put in gone to waste with a careless sentence. If you feel an excuse coming, restrain yourself!

2. **The Boring Bio**. 'Hi everyone, how are you doing? My name is ___ and before I start I'm going to run through my full CV in an attempt to convince you that I'm worth listening to.'

    What's wrong? Delivering your life history is not what you were brought into the room for. Providing context and experience can be very useful when done correctly, but not like this!

3. **The Speedy Spoiler**. 'Today I'm going to spend the next 15 minutes telling you about why we should do *insert point here*.'

    What's wrong? Delivering the talk's takeaway in the first sentence negates the rest of the presentation. You might as well skip straight to the Q and A after this opener: at least it will prevent your audience being talked at for 15 minutes!

The questions you need to answer:

1.   Why should they listen?

'It's been a challenging quarter for our team. I'm sure hearing this is no surprise to any of you. But rather than being downbeat, I'm hopeful, because we've learned more about our business model in the last three months than we have in the last year.'

2.   What are we going to uncover?

'The next few minutes are about getting clarity on three things. Firstly, where we are right now in relation to the targets we set at the beginning of the year. Secondly, what these results teach us about our business. And finally, which of these lessons we need to act on now so that we can focus on building some much-needed momentum in the next quarter.'

3.   What do you need from them?

'So here's what's going to happen… Rather than speak for 15 minutes, I'm going to talk for 10 and then I'd like to use the final 5 minutes to get your input on my proposed next steps so we can make a decision today.'

Here's why it works

- The tone of the whole presentation is clear from the very first sentence. Attaching emotion to the agenda, something that is typically delivered with apathy, helps to create the sense of importance and urgency you need to get everyone in the room to tune in.

- Your timeslot isn't a target. Gift your audience back some time. It will force you to be more concise with your message and only share what is relevant. No doubt your audience will thank you on both counts.

- The word 'we' assumes a sense of togetherness. It's a subtle way of creating a connection with your audience.

- Agenda items are kept purposefully vague and restricted to a maximum of three points. This keeps curiosity high and ensures that the to-do list doesn't sap the life and energy from their soul.

- Q and As don't work because they lack purpose. What's more, leaders want you to lead. So empowering your audience from the first minute not only forces everyone in the room to engage, but it will also make your presentation more useful as a result.

Remember, this is about priming your audience for what you're about to share. In the Toolkit, you'll find a cheat sheet with three fail-safe ways to open your next presentation to help you take this to the next level (Tool 2).

Come the end of your opener, the tone has been set, everyone should know what to expect, and they believe that what they are about to hear is worth listening to.

2. THE BACKGROUND: SET THE SCENE

What not to do

It's easy to assume that most of the room will be aware of the important stuff already, especially if you've sent over a slide deck ahead of time. But that doesn't mean you can just dive straight in. The truth is, most of your audience won't have given your presentation a second's thought until you started talking, which means that despite their best intentions, their heads are probably still stuck in whatever they were doing before. Your job now is to bring everyone up to speed, so that any gaps in knowledge are covered, and everyone has the information needed to make it through the whole presentation without getting lost.

These are the most common traps that presenters fall into with their background section:

1. **They lack relevancy by going too macro**. Now is not the right time to be reminding everyone of the company's purpose or delivering some top-level overview about how the company has evolved over the years.

What's wrong? Now is the time to get specific by curating the details that the audience needs to know. Doing so will transport everyone in the room into the here and now so they understand where you're coming from.

2.   **They place emphasis on what they've done rather than what they've learned**. This isn't a performance review, so don't make it feel like one.

What's wrong? Talking about all the work you've done or sharing lots of data in the hope that you come across as knowledgeable about your subject will likely infuriate your audience. Remember, what your audience is really after are insights. Curate the information you're sharing so that it improves their understanding of the team/department/company's prospects and strategy.

The questions you need to answer:

1.   **Where are we right now (in relation to the objectives)?**

'This year, our goal is to hit £10m annual recurring revenue. This means we need to be growing at a rate of about 10% each month. We're three months in and we already find ourselves 5% behind where we hoped we would be.'

2.   How did we end up here?

'In January, we grew 6.5%, and this dropped down to just 2.6% in February. Then, in March, we grew by 16%.

So what happened here? Why did the year start so slowly? And what can we learn from March's results?

Well, the numbers I've just presented to you don't tell the full story.

The truth is, January and February's results were expected. They follow the same trend as previous years and based on these two months alone, we would be on track to hit our £10m target.

It's because of March's results that we find ourselves 5% behind and I have been working with Marketing, Sales and Ops to work out why.

It turns out that there are two factors at play here…

Insight 1: The first being that a bad review from a customer that went undetected and as a result went viral.

Insight 2: Secondly, and most importantly, has been the drop in our customer lifetime value since the price hike.'

Here's why it works

- Your objectives provide a common language. They give a definition of success that everyone in the room can understand regardless of their expertise. And by sharing how you're doing in relation to your objectives, you help your audience to determine how they should feel about where you are now.

- Enough detail is provided to further understanding without becoming overwhelming. What to share and what not to share becomes easier to decide on when you know that your audience is less concerned with what has happened than they are with the lessons that come from it.

- We arrive at the insights quickly. Each insight is delivered as a headline so it's easy for your audience to remember. If there are several insights, numbering them can help you and your audience to keep track of the presentation's flow.

- This structure is repeatable. For example, you might have several objectives you need to report on. In this instance, answer the question 'Where are we right now?' for each of them, then choose the most relevant one to your presentation's purpose to deep dive into with the 'How did we end up here?' question.

- The insights are weighed in order of importance (with the most important last). This sets your audience up to be as engaged as possible for the next section of your presentation. It's important to note that the insights that you arrive at can be both positive and negative. Leadership needs to know what works as well as what doesn't.

Come the end of the background section, your audience should have enough knowledge to be able to engage with your presentation topic.

3. THE PROBLEM: CREATE THE OPPORTUNITY

What not to do

Don't make the mistake of thinking that your presentation doesn't need to address a problem. It does, and your job is to work out what it is. Sometimes the problem will be obvious: a toxic culture, buggy tech, a talent shortage, or customer retention.

But when there are no obvious problems to share, many presenters make the mistake of skipping this section entirely, resulting in a presentation that is less useful, lacking in purpose and, worst of all, forgettable.

Once presenters have identified the problem, these are the most common traps they fall into.

1. **They play the blame game.** 'We're not getting the support we need in order to hit the targets that you've set. Everyone in the team is exhausted and I'm having to work overtime fielding complaints from dissatisfied members of the team who are fed up and thinking of leaving.'

    What's wrong? It might be a powerful case, but it's also confrontational. The framing of your problems is critical to creating buy-in.

2. **The significance of the problem is assumed.** 'Our customers are leaving us. Let me tell you what I think we should do to ensure that they stay.'

    What's wrong? While the implications of what you share in this section might be clear to you, they won't be clear to everyone else, so you need to make sure you connect the dots.

The questions you need to answer:

1. What is holding us back?

'The price hike was unavoidable, but the impact it has already had on our customer retention figures is very concerning.'

2. **Why can't we stay here?**

'If things continue as they are, it's not just going to slow down growth, it's going to stop it completely. Come the end of the year, we will be lucky to hit 50% of what we had hoped to achieve.

But it's not just our targets that are going to suffer, our ability to retain our sales team will too. Many are already expressing frustration at the customer exodus and it wouldn't surprise me if our competitors, two of whom we know are actively recruiting in this field, start making moves to poach our talent.

In short, these are the two most pressing issues we need to tackle in order for us to keep growing at the rate we have planned.

The good news is that it's not too late to get back on track, provided we act now.'

Here's why it works

- Leaders are motivated by two things: frustration and fear. Igniting these emotions is critical if you want to influence them.

- No blame has been passed. As a result, the audience is still on your side and engaged. And framing your concerns as a peer rather than someone who is presenting up gives your message even more weight. You are speaking as one of them.

- Both the problem and its consequences are clear. By approaching the knock-on effects from different angles (here from a financial and a talent perspective) you are increasing the problem's relevancy and urgency.

- All solutions have been withheld, for now. Your audience needs to *feel* what is at stake before they can be influenced. The more frustrated with the problem they feel, the more likely they are to act (and fast).

- With the very last sentence, the audience is offered a glimmer of hope, incentivising them to listen to the next section of your presentation.

TIP

If you find yourself with no problem to share then turn your attention to pre-empting the problems that haven't happened yet. What are the challenges that lie ahead? Where could things go wrong? What needs to happen in order to maintain growth? Foresight is an enviable leadership trait and this is your opportunity to show it.

Come the end of the problem section, your audience shouldn't just understand the problem, they should be emotionally invested in it.

4. THE SOLUTION: REVEAL THE VISION

What not to do

Emotionally, we've taken the audience down into the pit of the problem, and now they need to be taken to a place of relief, hope and maybe even excitement. For that to happen, it will require a noticeable change in tone from you, but mid-presentation this can be easy to forget. Remember, communication is a transference of feelings. This means that the delivery of this section needs to reflect how you want your audience to feel.

These are the most common traps that presenters fall into here:

1. **Jumping straight into the how without providing the where**. As tempting as it might be to go straight into how these problems can be solved, the first thing your audience needs is clarity on the vision.

    What's wrong? Failure to set a clear direction will result in a confused audience that is highly unlikely to buy-in to the solutions that you're proposing. This is an opportunity to reset expectations and, if needed, share a new definition of success to be worked towards.

2. **Presenting the ideas in a disorganised way**. If your solution is multifaceted, ensuring that it is presented systematically is going to be critical.

    What's wrong? All too often, the solution is presented illogically without any thought being put into making it easy for the audience to follow.

3. **Falling back into the problem**. It is so easy to find yourself revisiting the problems you've already mentioned.

    What's wrong? This halts the momentum of your presentation and makes it very difficult to get back on track. It's time to leave the past behind and look ahead to how you can influence the future.

The questions you need to answer:

1. **Where do we need to go?**

    'The single most important thing we can do over the next four weeks is ensure we keep our current customers.

    If we can stop the leak now:

    1. Our customer lifetime value will increase.

    2. It will restore the team's confidence in the product.

3. We will create enough inbound leads to ensure we are back on track come the end of Q2.

The question is, how can we incentivise our customers to stay without devaluing what we currently offer or coming across as desperate and needy?!'

2. How do we get there?

'By getting them to buy into our future.

If the mass exodus has taught us anything, it's that the product we offer today is not a compelling enough reason for many of our customer base to stay.

But it will be in a few months' time, when we release the features that we have been working so hard on behind the scenes.

The reason our customers should stay with us is not because of what we offer now, but because of what we will offer in a few months' time.

I've been working with the team on a plan, and here's what we believe we should do:

1. Release an email to our whole customer base giving them a sneak peek of what we are releasing later this year. In there, include an opt-in for the customers who would be interested in getting early access in exchange for helping us test the features.

2. Then, to those who sign up, we follow up. Account management can book in calls and use this as an opportunity to re-establish relationships with our customers and empower them to be involved in our journey.

3. At the end of the call, we thank customers for their help and tell them about a referral scheme where they will get credit for themselves and every new customer they introduce. This will reduce our customer acquisition costs, create brand loyalty, and secure us some of the new leads we need to get back on track.'

Here's why it works

- The answer to each question is summed up in a single sentence. This ensures that you get to the point quickly and makes what you're sharing more memorable because you're jumping straight into the detail.

- After answering 'Where do we need to go?' comes the reasoning. Keeping it short, sweet and detail-free ensures that it packs a punch. On top of that, packaging your reasoning up in three short answers (aka the 'rule of three') is more compelling, easier to digest and more satisfying to say (see what I did there?!).

- Questions pique curiosity by empowering your audience to think. They help you talk *to* your audience rather than *at* them.

- The language used is definitive; it exudes confidence. Words like just, kind of, basically, quite, might etc. at best dilute the impact of your solution, and at worst plant a seed of doubt in your audience's mind.

- The 'how' is delivered step by step. As a result, it's much easier to follow, even for those who have a different primary area of expertise. If your presentation's purpose is to educate, you might decide to go into more detail in this section.

Come the end of your solution, your audience should have clarity on where you are going and how you intend to get there.

5. THE CONVINCER: BUILD THEIR CONFIDENCE

What not to do

For most presenters, this section doesn't exist. In their heads, the solution is where buy-in is created, so they progress straight to the close, confident that their job is done. But it's not. There might be a few who warm to your idea, but you won't have majority buy-in yet. Which is why this section is so important.

These are the most common traps that presenters fall into here:

1. **Setting yourself up to fail**. When you're invested in your solution, it can be easy to get carried away promising the world.

What's wrong? As tempting as it might be to talk best-case scenarios, managing your audience's expectations is critically important. Not only for this presentation, but for your next one too. Get this wrong and you could find yourself having to deliver even worse news the next time you meet. This is an opportunity to establish yourself as the reliable one.

2. **Labouring your own opinion.** By this point in the presentation, everyone has already heard plenty of your own reasons why you think your solution is going to work.

    What's wrong? Attempting to create buy-in by providing more of the same is not going to work. It's time for a change of tack by providing some evidence. This section is about saying 'don't just take my word for it. Look at this…!'

The questions you need to answer:

1. **Why is this going to work?**

    'When putting this plan together, the first question we asked ourselves was how many customers would need to opt in to the email for this project to be worthwhile? Based on the assumption that opting in is an indicator that they are intending to commit to for the next 12 months.

    The answer? 100.

And that's without any follow-up and relationship-building magic done by the account management team.

If 100 customers opt in, our customer lifetime value will restore to pre-price-hike levels.

The second question we asked was how likely is it that 100 of our customers will opt in?

Well, the last time we gave them the opportunity to test our new features early was two years ago.

Back then, and with a customer base that was half the size that it is now, 75 opted in, so it is reasonable to assume that this target can not only be hit, it can be surpassed.

Finally, we asked where those customers are now?

80% of them are still with us today.

They are our most loyal and engaged customers and they have a significant influence on our CLV.

The point is, those 100 customers won't just help us get back on track, they'll help us strengthen the foundations of a business that is growing at the rate we are.'

2.   Why is this the best way forward?

'It doesn't cost us anything other than time, it doesn't change our strategy, and implementing this now will give the team back the confidence they need to achieve the targets set at the beginning of the year.'

Here's why it works

- Repetition is used for emphasis. By repeating the most important number several times in the space of a couple of minutes, you are helping your audience stay focused on the goal. This is particularly useful when you're presenting data and have lots of numbers to share.

- The word 'magic' adds a bit of flair. It's not the word itself that's important, it's the fact that it brings a bit of your own personality into the presentation. Gone are the days of being overly formal when presenting. Don't be afraid to bring a bit of your own character into the language you use. It's more memorable and it will help you to connect with your audience.

- Detail is kept minimal. If your audience wants to dig into specific elements, they can do so in the Q and A.

- You've shown your workings. Pre-empting the questions your audience are likely to have been asking themselves doesn't just show a high level of emotional intelligence, it positions the presentation at their level. What's more, you've saved everyone time by significantly improving the usefulness of the Q and A to come.

- The final sentence re-emphasises the benefits (using the 'rule of three') and ensures that they stay front of mind.

If you're thinking about using data to give your solution credibility, check out my Data Storytelling Masterclass (Tool 3 in the Toolkit).

Come the end of your convincer, there should have been a noticeable shift in the room's warmth. The mood will have shifted from fear and frustration in the problem, to a mixture of hope and scepticism in the solution. A convincer done well should result in a mixture of relief and excitement.

6. THE CLOSE: FULFIL THE PURPOSE

What not to do

If the opener is about getting your audience to want to listen to your message, the close is about making sure it's remembered. The problem is, most presentations finish with a Q and A; a format which, while critically important, undoes all of the hard work you have put into your presentation unless you manage it correctly.

1. **Ending on the Q and A**. Do not let the final words of
    your presentation be 'Does anyone have any ques-
    tions?'

    What's wrong? No one has ever walked out of a pre-
    sentation thinking, 'Wow, that Q and A was amazing.'
    Always finish a presentation on your terms. It helps to
    convey your passion and your purpose.

2. **Repeating your agenda to recap**. 'Today we've looked
    at where we are relative to the targets we set at the
    beginning of the year, then we looked at what these
    results teach us…'

    What's wrong? The close is an opportunity to solidify
    takeaways, not waste your audience's time.

3. **Leaving the room feeling flat**. Your closing section will
    determine how your audience remembers the whole
    thing. If you want your presentation to leave a lasting
    impression and have a tangible impact, that will be
    determined by how you make them feel at the very end.

    What's wrong? It's likely that after the Q and A, the
    energy you worked hard to create in the solution and
    convincer will have disappeared. Your job is to re-ignite it.

The questions you need to answer:

1. **What would you like to achieve from the Q and A?**

   'Now feels like a good time to open the floor for any questions or comments you may have about what I've shared.

   There's lots to discuss, but from my side, it would be really useful to hear from anyone in the room that has experience implementing referral schemes like the one I mentioned.

   Q and A

   This has been really useful everyone, thank you. We've got time for one more question before I bring this to a close...'

2. **What is the one thing you need your audience to remember?**

   'If there is one thing I'd like you to take away from this presentation it is this: customer retention must become everyone's number-one priority over the next four weeks.'

3. **Why does it matter?**

   'If it does, the conversation we will be having three months from now will be a very different one.

Our CLV will be heading back in the right direction, we will have a stream of new leads to help us make up lost ground, and perhaps most importantly of all, overcoming this challenge will give our team the confidence boost they need to take us to that all-important £10m target, and that is incredibly exciting.

Thank you.'

Here's why it works

- The Q and A has a purpose. Being clear about an outcome that you'd like to achieve makes the transition into the Q and A easier. What's more, using words like 'comments' and 'discuss' make the format itself more flexible and more useful as a result.

- You stay in control of the Q and A. By pre-empting that there is time for one more question you ensure that you don't overrun and it allows you to take back control of the mic after the Q and A, so you can finish your presentation on your terms. You can always invite those with unanswered questions to follow up with an email.

- Your presentation's message is the takeaway. This way it stays front of mind. Notice how it's succinct – one sentence is enough. In most cases, repeating the problem will help you to convey a sense of urgency, while the solution will help you convey a sense of hope and excitement.

- A clear vision is delivered: a picture of the promised land! It evokes a sense of unity and strengthens the takeaway's importance. In the example, the rule of three was used for emphasis; repetition also works well here too.

- We finish on a feeling. What you say determines what your audience thinks; how you say it determines how your audience feels. This means you need to bring the emotion you want to evoke into your delivery. That's what will make sure it's remembered.

Tool 4 in the Toolkit is a cheat sheet with four ways to close a presentation with impact.

Come the end of your close, your message should be at the front of your audience's mind, along with the feeling that you decided was most appropriate for the content you delivered.

How to answer tricky questions off the cuff

---

et's briefly come back to the Q and A. If you're being asked some tough questions by your audience, here's a formula that will get you out of trouble and stop you from waffling.

Question:

> *'You mentioned earlier on in the presentation that a negative review went viral, how can we prevent this from happening in the future?'*

For the answer, think **PREP:**

Position: What do you think?

'Unfortunately, there is no fail-safe way to prevent it from happening.'

Reason: Why do you think that way?

'Social media has become one of the most popular ways to hold companies to account, and the quicker we grow, the more common negative viral reviews are going to become, and we need to get better at dealing with them.'

Example: What evidence have you got to support your point?

'In this particular incidence, the complaint came from an account that has over 50k followers, which is why it went viral. What made things trickier was that we weren't tagged in the post, and this meant that it went undetected for over 36 hours. As a result, by the time the social media team found out about it, it was too late. I spoke to the social media team yesterday and the good news is that the complaint has now been managed, and the post has been taken down. It has been an important lesson learned.'

Proposition: What should happen next?

'The most critical factor in managing these complaints is time. Since it happened, the team have responded quickly, and a system has been put in place to monitor a set of keywords related to our product. This will help us to detect any potential complaints 24/7, regardless of whether or not we have been tagged directly in the posts.'

WHY MOST PRESENTATIONS FLATLINE

At the heart of this structure is a principle that applies to every single type of presentation you will ever deliver:

Emotional contrast creates memories.

The problem with most presentations is they emotionally flatline and the audience struggles to connect with the speaker and the message as a result. A presentation needs both positive and negative moments in order for it to be an engaging and memorable experience.

If everything you share evokes the same emotional response, from the audience's perspective nothing will stand out because everything feels the same. It's emotional monotony, which, if we were to represent it in a graph, would look something like this:

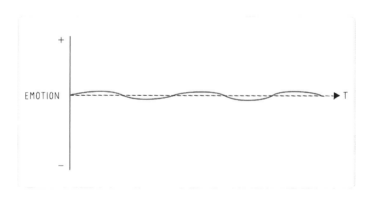

The structure we've looked at above ensures your audience is taken on a journey that enables them to experience both positive and negative emotions. This helps them to get passionate about whatever it is you're talking about. As a result, your audience's journey will look something like this:

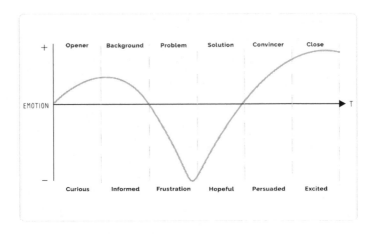

It is in the emotional contrast that the memories are created. The deeper you're able to get your audience to feel the problem, the higher you'll be able to leave them and the more impact your presentation will have as a result.

Don't just take my word for it, take Nobel-Prize-winning psychologist Daniel Kahneman's. He and his team spent years researching how we remember things that have happened to us. At the heart of our relationship between memory and experience is a cognitive bias known as the peak–end rule. Kahneman found that an experience's peak (the most intense point) and its end can significantly influence how we remember the experience as a whole.

For example, you attend a concert that has really poor sound quality, but your favourite song is played at the very end; as a result, you still remember the experience as a positive one. Or you are involved in a really tense football match and you score a goal (peak experience). This will impact the memory of the event as a whole.

If we can be intentional about the experience we create for the audience at the presentation's peak and its end, we can influence how they see the whole presentation.

HOW TO ALIGN YOUR STRUCTURE WITH YOUR PURPOSE

Irrespective of whether your presentation's purpose is to update, educate or persuade, the structure doesn't change. What distinguishes the purpose is the amount of time you dedicate to specific sections.

The very nature of an update means that you will dedicate most of your presentation to answering the question 'How did we end up here?' in the background section.

If the purpose of your talk is to educate, then deep-diving into the intricacies of the 'How do we get there?' question in the solution section of the talk is where you need to spend the most time.

When it comes to persuading, the most common mistake presenters make is in thinking that the buy-in happens in the solution. This isn't the case. It's by answering the question 'Why is this going to work?' in the convincer, so you'll need to spend the most time there.

The diagram below shows which section should be the main focus of your presentation, depending on the purpose.

This is the same whether you're presenting for 15 minutes or an hour.

UPDATE						
O	B	P	S	C	C	

EDUCATE						
O	B	P	S	C	C	

PERSUADE						
O	B	P	S	C	C	

TIP

—

One of the most common types of presentations you'll likely be asked to deliver is the weekly/monthly/ quarterly review.

In this case, use the background section to cover the time period just gone (e.g. Q2), the problem section to draw attention to what has been holding your results back right now, and the solution section to reveal where you plan to be at the end of the next time period (e.g. Q3).

Now you have this structure, it's about adapting it to suit the needs of the presentation you're delivering.

EXERCISE

Create a presentation outline

Now you understand the structure, it's time to spend 10 minutes creating a presentation outline. This will help to ensure that every section of your presentation is aligned with your purpose and the message you want to share.

What you don't want to do (and the mistake that most people make) is create your presentation by building a slide deck as you go. Slides have a nasty habit of sucking you into the detail before you've established the audience's journey (and you're going to get a slide deck template in the next section of the book).

Instead, map out your whole presentation on a single page using the Speedy Speech-Writing Framework on page 76 (Tool 5 in the Toolkit).

This will ensure that you avoid death by detail (saving you hours of unnecessary presentation prep), your audience doesn't get overwhelmed and your presentation's message doesn't get lost.

Summary of Part 1

By following the process outlined in Part 1, every presentation you deliver will be armed with a powerful purpose, a clear message and a compelling audience journey. Practise it a few times and it won't be long before it becomes second nature. You'll be able to create presentations in less time and with less stress.

At this point, you'll be ready to take your presentations to the next level by bringing in storytelling to give your insights even more impact. To give you a head start on this, check out Tool 6 in the Toolkit, a cheat sheet with eight powerful stories to start incorporating into your presentations.

In a nutshell, here's the process you want to follow when putting together a presentation.

1. PURPOSE	2. MESSAGE
UPDATE EDUCATE PERSUADE (CIRCLE AS APPROPRIATE)	THE POINT IS...

3. OPENER	4. BACKGROUND
1. WHY SHOULD THEY LISTEN? 2. WHAT ARE WE GOING TO UNCOVER? 3. WHAT DO YOU NEED FROM THEM?	1. WHERE ARE WE RIGHT NOW (IN RELATION TO THE OBJECTIVES)? 2. HOW DID WE END UP HERE?

5. PROBLEM	6. SOLUTION
1. WHAT IS HOLDING US BACK? 2. WHY CAN'T WE STAY HERE?	1. WHERE DO WE NEED TO GO? 2. HOW DO WE GET THERE?

7. CONVINCER	8. CLOSER
1. WHY IS THIS GOING TO WORK? 2. WHY IS THIS THE BEST WAY FORWARD?	1. WHAT WOULD YOU LIKE TO ACHIEVE FROM THE Q AND A? 2. WHAT IS THE ONE THING YOU NEED YOUR AUDIENCE TO REMEMBER? 3. WHY DOES IT MATTER?

PART 2

CONNECTION

Your job is to make the audience care

Your audience's most valuable commodity is their attention. Without it, we have nothing, which is why being able to create a connection with our audience is so important. Our job as presenters is to get them to spend their attention on us.

The problem is, your audience has got a long list of things that they would rather be doing than listening to you!

Blunt? Perhaps... but going into every presentation with this in mind will stand you in great stead because it is up to you to make your audience care. Your job is to take them from a place of apathy to action.

The presenters who are unable to connect sap the life and energy from their audience's soul. It was one of the biggest frustrations from the leaders that I interviewed for this book:

'I get frustrated by presenters who are monotonous and just go through the motions. They have a terrible impact on the morale for those who listen – they are toxic.'

'Reading out slides and looking at the screen rather than the audience is a sure fire way of making me drift off.'

'Overformality. Boards are mistaken for scary robots that operate on an input > process info > output basis and thus the presentations are void of emotion. We want to be made to feel something!'

And you thought I was blunt!

So the ability to connect is important. It's also something that you can learn. Contrary to popular belief, it's not a skill that's reserved for the lucky few who are 'natural' entertainers. Nor is it just for those who have 'interesting' topics to present about.

Connecting with your audience will enable you to deliver memorable presentations that will impress the people who matter, and it will give you an unfair advantage in the world of work.

How to speak so people want to listen

I once worked with a beatboxer who told me that our voice is the most powerful instrument in the world. How we use our voice as presenters has never been more important. With many of us spending as much time presenting to screens on video calls as we do in person, how we sound has become even more important than how we look. Audience members spend more time listening to presentations than they do watching them.

And that's important because while our words might determine what people think, how we communicate them will determine what people feel.

As listeners, we're very good at picking up on the subtle nuances of how other people speak. Words alone aren't enough. How the words are being said helps us to sense how deeply someone cares about and believes in what they're saying, as well as what they feel about it. Every time we pick up the phone, we accurately interpret how someone's day is going from how they say hello.

But this brilliant skill of ours is a subconscious one. Ask someone to explain exactly how to convey emotion using only the voice and they'd probably find it quite challenging to do so.

As presenters, the way we communicate can change when we find ourselves in high-pressure situations. Our natural intonation gets stripped and sanitised because we feel flustered or we're trying too hard to remember our lines or read from our notes. When there's a disconnect between what we're trying to say and how we say it, it can result in our message being misinterpreted or dismissed as unimportant.

Some speak too fast and frustrate their audiences by being difficult to understand. Others, who come across as confident in one-to-one situations, seem to lose their gravitas when they present; their words carry less weight. And then there are those who struggle with monotony – the ultimate audience off-switch.

You can have the best message in the world, but if you're not engaging to listen to, it will fall on deaf ears.

There are four ways you can use your voice to enhance your level of engagement and increase the impact you have when you present to ensure that your message lands. I call them the 4Ps: pitch, pace, power and pause.

PITCH

Pitch is one of the biggest factors in determining how confident you sound. It's about your vocal range – how high and how low your voice goes and when.

When we are under pressure, pitch is often the first thing that will change. There's no need for overanalysis here. The most important thing to become aware of is what happens to your voice at the end of a sentence.

In situations where we are feeling nervous, stressed, intimidated, or when we are unsure of our message, there are two traps we tend to fall into.

Inflecting up

Inflecting up often signals that we are asking a question, so when we do it outside of this context it gives the impression we're either questioning ourselves or that we don't really believe in what we're saying.

What's more, while we might associate upward inflection with asking a question, the truth is it tends to only be used in situations where we are unsure of the outcome or we are looking for certainty from others.

'Hello? Is anyone there?'

Imagine proposing to someone while inflecting up at the end of that all-important sentence...

'Will you marry me?!'

'Err... no thanks, you're not confident enough.'

In short, if you want to sound confident, make sure you don't inflect up at the end of your sentences!

Inflecting across

If you keep your voice at a consistent pitch all the way through, it makes you sound like you're on autopilot and you don't care. It's like you're just going through the motions and you will lose the human element of your presentation as a result.

This happens when you read your notes verbatim or fail to connect with your subject matter. Both of which we'll cover later in this book (pages 101 - 108).

Here's what you should do instead…

Inflecting down

Inflecting down at the end of a sentence signals that you have confidence in what you're saying and it will enable you to deliver your message with more weight as a result.

The most important ingredient between a speaker and their audience is trust. If they get the sense that you don't believe in what you're presenting, then there is no chance of your message landing.

Say this sentence out loud:

'I like chocolate.'

Notice how the final syllable inflects down? That's what we're aiming for.

Now try saying it again, but this time inflect up at the end. It's surprisingly difficult and requires vast amounts of concentration (or at least it does for me). It also sounds much more uncertain.

Use pitch to increase your engagement. If you want your words to carry more weight, inflect down at the end of your sentences.

PACE

Pace is one of the most effective ways of expressing passion. It's the speed at which you speak.

When we are under pressure, the adrenaline of the occasion can cause us to speak faster than we would normally.

A common misconception is that speaking fast is a problem and that in order to be an effective presenter you must speak slowly. But the real problem is speaking at a consistent pace throughout your presentation.

It's essentially a form of hypnotism. Great for meditation, sleep stories and shipping forecasts, but bad for everything else. It's like taking your audience on a journey that is stuck at 40mph all the way.

The secret to using pace effectively in your presentations is to speed up to create excitement and slow down for impact. This will help give your presentations a more natural, conversational feel. Like you were catching up with a friend in a coffee shop.

To see this in action, watch Carla Harris's TED talk (Tool 7 in the Toolkit).

I give my clients access to a tool that analyses recordings of the presentations they deliver so we can measure the improvement in their verbal, visual and vocal delivery. I used it to analyse Harris's talk, and what you will notice from the graph is that her pace is constantly changing.

As a result, she is incredibly easy to listen to as a presenter.

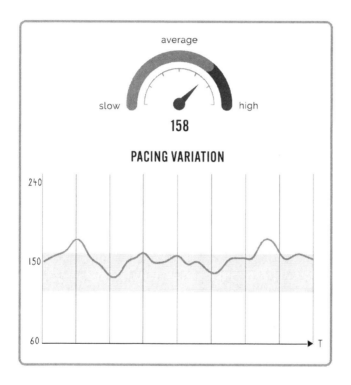

Vary your pace: speed up for excitement, slow down for impact.

The two most important parts of your presentation are the opener and the close. So drop your pace by 15% in both. This will give your audience time to tune in to your voice without becoming overwhelmed and ensure that your message lands with as much clarity as possible.

POWER

Power can change the energy in the room. It's about your volume: how loudly or softly you speak.

Power is often misused. Some fall into the trap of projecting their voice for the duration of their presentation, resulting in the audience feeling like they're being talked at rather than talked to. Others think that increasing their volume increases the importance of the point they're making.

Yes, you need to speak at a level that ensures everyone in the room can hear you without having to strain to do so, but the most engaging presenters are constantly changing the power of their voice to ensure that their message lands with impact.

The secret here is to increase your volume when you need to give your audience a burst of enthusiasm, and speak softly when you need your audience to really concentrate on the point you're making.

A great example of using power effectively is Michelle Obama's speech at the 2016 Democratic Convention (see Tool 8 in the Toolkit). At the time of writing, it's her most-watched speech on YouTube. Her job that day was to get the audience excited.

So did she power pose her way on stage, beating her chest like a caricature of some inspirational speaker?

No.

She started softly. Her audience was already excited to see her speak, so she wanted to settle them down to help them tune in to the message she wanted to land. Then she increased her volume to build the energy up, before dropping it back down so she could finish on a crescendo.

If she had projected her voice the whole time, there would be nowhere for her power to go; without the moments of softness, the crescendo wouldn't exist. Here's a graph from my presentation analysis platform, MicDrop Analytics, showing the wide variations in her volume during that speech:

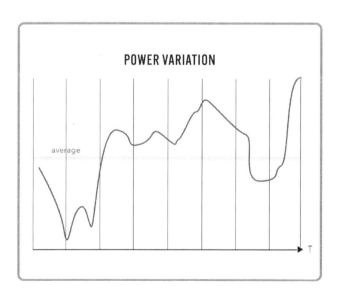

Vary your power: increase your power for passion, and decrease it for importance.

In the opening section of your talk, contrast your delivery style with the energy level of the room. If your audience's energy levels are low, your job is to give the room an injection of enthusiasm by increasing your volume. If the energy is already high, a calmer delivery style will help your audience settle so that you can take them on the journey you want them to experience (like Michelle Obama).

In the closing section of your talk, your power will depend on how you want your audience to feel. If you want them to feel calm and reassured, then softening your voice will help to create the energy you need. If you want them to feel excited and inspired to act, give them a burst of energy by increasing your volume.

TIP

___

If you find yourself presenting in a scenario where you are only invited to the part of the meeting where you're presenting, you will not have a feel for the room's mood. If this meeting has been running for several hours (often the case with board meetings, for example), you need to be mindful of audience fatigue. If it's been a long day for them, the energy will be low and it's your job to raise it. This is where the information that you gather from the email questionnaire on page 32 can be incredibly helpful. If in doubt, up the power for the opener. Enthusiasm always wins.

PAUSE

Pauses are a presenter's way of commanding the audience's attention. These pauses are deliberate: they're used to hold the audience in suspense for a moment, and using them shows that the presenter has complete control of the room, like the conductor of an orchestra. Unfortunately, all too often they are underused and overlooked, which is a shame given how easy they are to use.

Most presenters either don't pause at all, or if they try to, they don't hold the pause for long enough to create the desired effect on the audience. This is because it feels much longer for you than it does for them.

The purpose of a pause is to heighten the emotional experience. Without pauses, the impact of your presentations will be limited. With them, you will unlock higher highs and lower lows for your audience, making both your presentation and your message more memorable as a result.

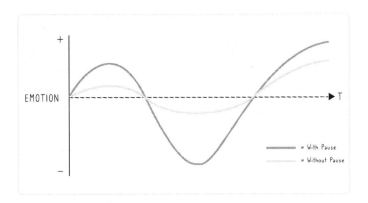

While standing in front of a group of people and holding a silence can feel excruciatingly uncomfortable at first, the benefits are more than worth it. Not least the fact that learning how to be comfortable with silence is the cure for anyone who suffers from needlessly uttering filler words like ums and ahs.

So how long does a pause need to be in order for it to have an impact? Anything less than a second and your audience won't have been given enough time to feel its effects.

Beyond that, it's very dependent on the occasion and the importance of the point you're trying to make. With practice, you'll learn to find a balance that works well for you and your own presentation style.

A simple trick that I use is to say to myself 'this moment is mine' to fill the pause.

The three most effective places to use pauses in a presentation

1. Before and after your first sentence.

Most people rush into starting their presentations because their fight or flight response gets the better of them. Taking the time to hold a pause before you start presenting shows confidence, gives you the chance to centre yourself, and signals to your audience that you're about to start and their full attention is required.

> *(Pause) 'It's been a challenging quarter*
> *for our team.' (Pause)*

2. After asking a question.

We mentioned how incorporating questions into your presentation can help you to feel like you're having a conversation with your audience (albeit a silent one). The secret is to ask questions that get your audience thinking – ones where the answer isn't immediately obvious.

'The question is, how can we incentivise our customers to stay without devaluing what we currently offer or coming across as desperate and needy?!' (Pause)

Pausing straight after the question gives your audience a chance to consider an answer. It makes them active participants in your presentation rather than passive listeners.

3. Before and after delivering a 'power statement'.

There are normally one or two sentences in every section of the presentation that you know you need to land. It might be an insight that you want your audience to remember, the moral of a story you're going to share, or the answer to this question:

Why am I telling you this?

I call these sentences 'power statements'. Sandwiching power statements with a pause is the most effective way to make these sentences stand out.

(Pause) 'Our biggest problem has been the drop in our customer lifetime value since the price hike.' (Pause)

The first pause is designed to create anticipation for what you're about to say. It also acts as a kind of life raft by helping members of the audience who had lost concentration to re-engage. The second pause gives your audience a chance to reflect on and feel the consequences of the point you've just made. The important thing to note here is that it is the pauses that make the sentence powerful. Without them, these words will carry the same amount of weight as everything else.

TIP

———

Choose the most important sentence of each section to deliver as a power statement. The pauses provide a jolt of emotional energy and give your audience a chance to feel your statement's impact. Doing this increases the level of engagement and literally brings life into your presentation – it gives your presentation a pulse.

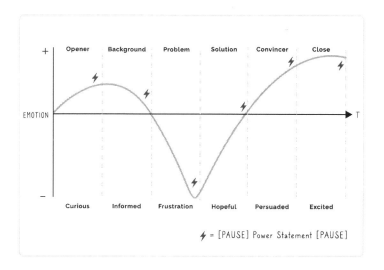

⚡ = [PAUSE] Power Statement [PAUSE]

EXERCISE

Record and upload a 1-minute video to MicDrop Analytics

One of the very first things my clients have to do when they enrol in one of my programmes or join MicDrop, my public speaking club, is record a video of themselves presenting to camera using my presentation analysis platform. And to thank you for reading my book, I'd like to give you the opportunity to do the same.

You will get real-time feedback on your content, voice and body – from how effectively you vary your pace, to the length of your pauses and how many ums and ahs you use when you present.

Self-awareness is a critical component of every presenter's toolkit. When you know where you're at right now, you'll be able to pinpoint which areas you need to start working on.

Simply go to Tool 9 in the Toolkit to get access to the platform. Then, upload a pre-recorded video of yourself presenting or record one live on the platform itself. When you sign in, you will find instructions on how to use the platform and what to look out for from a delivery perspective.

How to look natural when everyone is staring at you

―――――

I t's not just our voice that changes when we have to communicate in high-pressure situations. Our bodies do too.

The reason why we often feel uncomfortable on stage is because we have entered a heightened state of awareness. Every single part of our body feels strange, as though it doesn't belong there.

A great example of this was when I was getting my teeth cleaned by the hygienist the other week. At one point, the hygienist asked me to move my tongue. Until then, I'd not given my tongue's position a second thought. But suddenly, I was so aware of it! Everywhere I tried to put my tongue felt strange – it didn't feel right!

You might now be thinking about where your tongue is positioned. Perhaps it's touching the roof of your mouth, or maybe the tip is touching the back of your bottom teeth? Whatever you do, don't think about it too much or you'll struggle to find a comfortable home!

When we present, this sensation of heightened awareness can be felt in every part of our body. It makes us tense up, and prevents us from connecting with our audience because we come across awkwardly.

But I've got some good news. There are some very simple things you can do to ensure that you look as engaging as you now sound. And best of all, they're things that you already do naturally everyday. So don't overcomplicate it, just make sure you include them when you present.

SMILE

Your audience is a reflection of you. This means that if your audience is apathetic, it's because you're lacking energy. If everyone in the room is stony-faced, it's because you are so engrossed in getting the job done well that the last thing on your mind is making sure you greet your audience with an expression that makes them warm to you.

You'd be amazed at the power of a smile. When you're presenting to a bunch of senior leaders who spend their lives dealing with problem after problem, it will be an unexpected but very welcome addition to the room. It also gives the impression that you want to be there, even when you don't!

That's not to say that you want to plaster a beaming smile on your face that stays there from the moment you take the floor to the moment you sit down. But making a smile your first and last impression certainly isn't going to do any harm.

I once got told that we smile 33% of the time we think we are smiling.

It turns out there's no truth in that statistic whatsoever, but it's always stuck with me. The reason you should make a point of smiling is because it's contagious. Every smile you get back from the audience is a bit of encouragement and permission for you to be yourself.

MAKE EYE CONTACT

To get that smile from your audience, you're going to need to look at them. We know that eye contact is essential to building trust, and if you're presenting to a relatively small group you should be able to make sure that everyone in the room feels like you're talking to them. That doesn't mean you need to work your way individually along each row; that would be weird! But it is important to address every part of a room, and I highly recommend picking out several individuals across an audience to address specifically the most. Making eye contact is particularly effective when you're delivering your power statements.

USE YOUR HANDS

There's something about being able to see another person's hands that I think is an important part of building trust. When we feel uncomfortable, our natural response is to hide our hands. We cross our arms, put our hands behind our backs or put one hand in our pocket, thinking that if we have at least one hand out, we might be able to get away it!

So where should we put our hands? I think it's less about putting them somewhere and more about giving them something to do. Like our voice, our hands are an instinctive part of the way we communicate – I read about a study a few years back that found people who are born blind use hand gestures when they speak.

So keep it simple. Keep your elbows by your side and your hands in front of you – you should be able to see them in the lower third of your vision. Then let your hands help you communicate the point you're trying to make, just like you already do when you're chatting to friends over drinks.

Communication is a transference of feelings

Now I appreciate that there's a lot to take in. You might feel you've got enough to be thinking about in the middle of a presentation without also remembering to pause for the right length of time, and use your hands, and make sure your sentences inflect downwards, and so on. How on earth are you meant to incorporate all of that?!

By connecting with your passion.

When you are catching up with a friend, putting the world to rights, there's a good chance you do every single one of these things automatically. The skills themselves are instinctive.

One of the most telling pieces of feedback I got from my interviews for this book was:

'You wouldn't have been given the job if you didn't care. So why aren't you showing it?!'

Your audience wants you to bring passion into your presentations. Now, what your audience probably doesn't realise is that they are wearing an expression on their face that suggests their pet cat has just died, or worse still, you killed their cat! So it's no wonder the atmosphere in the room can cause you to tense up, especially if all your focus is on making sure you don't forget your words (more on that in the next section of the book). But the truth is, it is not your audience's responsibility to make you feel comfortable enough to express yourself. It's yours.

Communication is a transference of feelings.

There's a very important question you should ask yourself just before every presentation you deliver:

Why does this presentation matter to you?

While it's a big question, it's not one that you need to over-think.

In the lead up to a presentation, we can lose perspective on what's important. Suddenly, the things we care about are:

- not forgetting our words

- making sure we cover all the content we had planned

- not making a fool of ourselves

- doing the best job we possibly can

- what our audience thinks of what we present

- the way we present, etc.

In other words, everything that makes us less comfortable and more awkward. This is why it's so important to step back and get some perspective.

IS IT ABOUT THE OUTCOME OR THE OPPORTUNITY TO HELP?

For some (and I include myself in this category), the passion is for the outcome: the ripple effect, the opportunity to effect change on a larger scale. When you know that what you're going to present will influence the bigger picture, it's hard not to get excited about what it is you're going to share.

For others, it's more about the opportunity to help others; something that is very easy to forget when you find yourself preparing a slide deck at 11pm the night before. Every presentation you deliver is a gift. It is an opportunity to serve and it is selfless. Reframing your presentation in this way can turn it into something you're looking forward to, rather than something you're dreading.

Getting clear on which one of these camps you fall into will give you the sense of purpose you need to find and channel the energy and passion required to get your message across.

CONNECT WITH IT, THEN CHANNEL IT

Take a moment just before every presentation to bring that passion to the front of your mind. You've done the prep, so this is the time to focus on energy, not a perfectly prepared message. Then channel that energy to ensure that what you want to say isn't just heard, it is felt.

I recently worked with the head of recruitment for a software engineering company. His name was Andy, and he enrolled in one of my coaching programmes because he wanted to present with more influence, particularly when the stakes of the presentation were high.

The business was scaling and he was in charge of growing the team. The problem was, for every person his department recruited, a current employee was poached by their competitors. So rather than helping the team to grow, in reality, he was plugging a leaking bucket.

During one of our coaching sessions, Andy mentioned that he was due to deliver an 'update' to the board next month and wanted to use the opportunity not just to make them aware that the team wasn't growing, but to persuade them that this was not going to change unless they increased salaries company-wide.

In our session the following week, we rehearsed his presentation. He made a brilliant business case for increasing salaries. Or he would have if he'd just sent me the script via email. From a content perspective it had everything it needed:

- Research that categorically proved poor remuneration was the problem.

- A solution that contained three different sources of money that the business could use to increase salaries without impacting the bottom line.

- A vision of how quickly the company could grow once they increased salaries.

The problem was that I was struggling to concentrate. My mind kept wandering off... There's definitely something missing on my to-do list, what is it? What am I going to cook tonight? I've not listened to a word he's said for the last two minutes, how on earth do I frame my feedback?!

If I had been the decision maker in the boardroom that day, my response would have been, 'Thanks for giving us a heads up, Andy. Let's monitor this over the next six months and we can review again after that.'

Apathy.

His delivery lacked the urgency that he desperately felt. He wanted things to change quickly, but the way it came across undermined the importance of the problem.

So I was honest. I told him that I kept switching off and that I could barely hear the problem, let alone feel it. Then I asked him, 'Why does this presentation matter to you?' His reply: 'Because my team are demoralised and they feel like they're fighting a losing battle. Our business has become a training ground that our competitors are capitalising on.'

When he said it, I could feel his frustration. So I told him to show it.

It turns out that for Andy, while the outcome of a salary increase was important, for him this was really about speaking on behalf of his team. This presentation was an opportunity to help them.

From that moment on, showing passion became his presentation's only success criteria. When the day came to deliver the presentation for real, he walked out of the room knowing that he'd been heard and had done everything he could for his team.

An hour later, he received a message from his manager praising the quality of his presentation. The first time that had ever happened in his career.

Not only that, he walked out of that presentation knowing that he had done everything he could. He now walks into those meetings with the confidence that not only can he speak at their level, but that his opinion has value.

YOUR PASSION IS YOUR PRESENTATION'S LIFE RAFT

Four weeks ago, I started a course designed to help the leaders of a SaaS company prepare for their next company-wide meeting (aka all-hands meeting). The first live workshop is always the hardest because it's your first time with the team. I'd been given a list of attendees, but when I logged on, there was a name that I very much recognised that hadn't been included on the original list. It was the CEO!

That sort of thing doesn't normally phase me these days, but for some reason, on this particular occasion it caught me completely off-guard. I started to sweat, my brain went into overload and I suddenly found myself very short of breath.

Luckily, just before the call I'd taken a minute to channel my passion. And as someone who thrives on outcomes, for me, this was about getting the team ready to deliver the best all-hands meeting in their company's history.

The old me would have played it safe by doubling down on my notes and sticking to the plan. But because my passion was front of mind, rather than opening with what I'd prepared beforehand (which, on reflection, wasn't as good!), I took a deep breath and opened with that instead. I paused, I smiled. I made a point of looking into the camera and then I opened with, 'Over the course of the next six weeks, my job is simple. To help you deliver the best all-hands meeting in your company's history.'

COMMUNICATION IS A TRANSFERENCE OF FEELINGS

Then after that I paused again. That opening sentence grounded me; it reminded me of how much I cared about the outcome and helped forge a connection with everyone on the call. The session couldn't have gone any better. I know that because the CEO not only booked into his one-to-one coaching call later that week, but he's also turned up to the three sessions we've had since then.

The point is, if you end up with a curveball that throws you off track, fall back on your passion. Remember the feedback I shared earlier in the chapter – the thing that leaders really want is to see you care. That's what you need to show when you find yourself feeling confronted or intimidated by the people in the room. By focusing on the passion, you will help your message to land.

Slides: the single biggest threat to your presentations (until now)

———

Contrary to popular belief, slides are the single biggest threat to delivering an engaging presentation. They are a connection killer. Used incorrectly (like most people do), they steal the attention away from you, what you're saying and the emotional journey you're trying to create.

You can come up with all the excuses you like as to why your presentation needs a slide deck, but the real reason is because it gives you something to hide behind. It helps you stay on track, and it's something to fall back on when you forget your words. But your audience doesn't want a report, they want a presentation.

Slide decks are a crutch. And you will only truly reach your full presenting potential when you can learn to present without one.

After I give this pep talk to my clients, they often come back with, 'But I can't just turn up to a presentation without a slide deck. It will look like I've not prepared!'

I promise you this: 30 seconds after nailing your opener, they'll think you've done more work than everyone else and they'll be fully engaged.

The most surprising insight from the interviews I conducted for this book was how little tolerance everyone had for the poor use of slides. If you presented to this lot without any slides, they'd probably thank you! I'd list some of the comments, but to be completely honest, there are too many to choose from and they all say the same thing:

'Stop reading from your slides.'

'Stop overloading them with detail.'

'Stop looking at the laptop/projector screen and start engaging with me!'

End of chapter!

Or it would be, except for the fact that when used sparingly, slides can supercharge the connection you have with your audience.

But before you crack open your presentation software and spend hours putting together a slide deck that's going to make your presentation worse, ask yourself:

What can slides say that I can't?

WARNING: If you can't get your message across without slides, it means there's a problem with your message. Spend your time on that instead.

THE GOLDEN RULES OF ENGAGING SLIDES

Rule 1: Use a blank slide the most

This cleverly designed slide tells your audience: 'There is nothing to see here, so get back to looking at me!' A black slide gives the impression you've turned the projector off, and it is a game changer!

For example, say you only need to incorporate slides into your background and solution sections. When you're communicating the problem, the background slides are no longer relevant, and putting in slides for the sake of it dilutes the impact of the ones you do need.

This is where the blank slide comes into its own. Aim to use it for at least half of your presentations.

Rule 2: Make the slide background dark

White slide backgrounds look distinctly amateurish and set a poor tone. Switching to a dark background with a contrasting colour for your text is by far the simplest way to take your slide design to the next level. Not only that, it will prevent the screen from becoming this giant, bright light which our eyes can't help but be drawn to.

Dark backgrounds help our audience's eyes to relax and ensure that you are the most interesting thing to look at.

Rule 3: Keep to one message per slide max

If a slide isn't digestible in a second, it needs to be simplified. Time spent trying to decipher a slide's meaning is time spent not looking at or listening to you.

Every slide should contain a maximum of one message.

This means that lists, graphs and tables are banned from your slide decks. Or at least they are until you've learned how to harness the power of contrast. Used correctly, contrast will direct your audience's focus to the exact thing you want them to see.

Here are some examples of this technique in action:

Lists

From: to:

1: Use a blank slide the most	1: Use a blank slide the most
2: Make the background dark	2: Make the background dark
3: Keep to one message per slide max	**3: Keep to one message per slide max**

Tables

From: to:

Q1 % Growth

	Jan	Feb	Mar
Actual	6.5	2.6	16
Planned	6.1	2.9	20
Difference	0.4	0.3	-4

Q1 % Growth

	Jan	Feb	Mar
Actual	6.5	2.6	16
Planned	6.1	2.9	20
Difference	0.4	0.3	**-4**

Graphs

From: to:

Rule 4: Avoid animation at all costs!

Adding animation to your slide deck is a complete waste of your time. Instead, create a separate slide for each animation to manually create the 'appear' effect. For example:

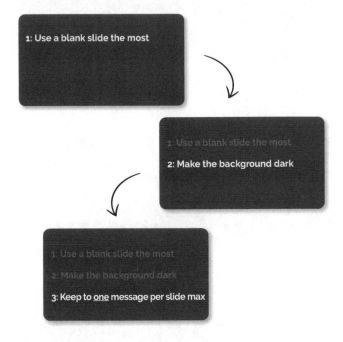

The quickest way to do this is to create the complete version of the slide and then work backwards by duplicating the slide and deleting/fading out appropriately. This will save you lots of awkward flicking through your slides if you skip forward by accident mid-presentation.

Rule 5: Lead with your words, not with your slides

Remember, you are competing with your slide deck for your audience's attention. This means that the timing of your slides is critical to the success of your talk. The mistake most presenters make is to put up the slide they are about to talk about, and then they talk about it.

When the slide comes first, you are placing more importance on your visual aid than on what you're saying.

Instead, prepare your audience for what they're about to see by making your points, then revealing the slide.

This will ensure each slide delivers a message and that your audience's curiosity is peaked when you give them the chance to see it. A simple way to do this is to give each slide a trigger word. When you say the word, you present the slide.

A perfect example of leading with your words, not with your slides, comes in the first three minutes of a rather humorous TED talk by Tim Urban (Tool 12 in the Toolkit).

There are two things he does particularly well here. Firstly, his slide timing allows the story he is telling to flow seamlessly – his words and his slides are in harmony. Secondly, his slides are so simple that as soon as you've digested the slide, your attention turns back to him.

This is the gold standard for you to work towards!

TIP

___

Create a lite version of an information-heavy deck for the presentation itself

Sometimes, the devil is in the details and decisions can't be made without them. This is particularly true when money is at stake. I spoke to the managing partner of a leading UK Venture Capital firm recently who all too often is on the receiving end of a deck that is packed full of information. They said that they would much prefer the presenter to use a lite version of the slide deck for the presentation itself and then follow up with (or even send in advance) the full version for them to digest in their own time.

Another direct quote from my interviews:

'Bonus point [if the presenter] has spoken to me or provided some content and context beforehand so I had the chance to give it some pre-thought and come "armed with a view".'

EXERCISE

10x the effectiveness of your presentation slides

Tool 10 in the Toolkit is a video that will show you exactly how to harness the power of contrast when designing your slides. Watch it and implement it!

Along with the video, I've created a beautifully designed slide deck template (Tool 11) to save you a load of time on slide design. Simply download the file and make it your own.

Hack your video presence for remote presentations

The ability to deliver compelling presentations online is no longer a nice to have, it's a need to have. There is a tremendous opportunity to differentiate yourself from your peers if you are able to nail this medium.

The standard of the average online presentation is catastrophically poor – the working world seems to be plateauing at a forgettable 4/10. What an opportunity you have to raise the bar and deliver something memorable!

Online audience apathy is rife. But it needn't be.

If there is one thing you need to know about an online audience, it's that in most cases, the 'room' will be void of energy. Especially if everyone is dialling in separately.

Remember, you might be the first human contact they've had in hours.

This means that your job is to up the energy. Here's how to do it.

BEFORE THE PRESENTATION

Far too many people present on video sat slumped back in their chairs like Jabba the Hutt, in a room that looks so dark it makes them look more like a serial killer than a leader. It's time to reset the bar.

Stand

Stand up and position your laptop so that the webcam is adjusted to eye height. If you don't have a standing desk, short-term solutions (both of which I have used) include: using an ironing board (aka portable desk) with a stack of books on it, or a chair on the table. I highly recommend investing in a £30 or so standing desk. The one I have been using for the last five years is from Lavolta (give them a google – I don't get commission from them, but frankly I should).

Now, before we move on, I should address the question you're really thinking.

'Do I really have to stand up?'

Yes, you do. Why? Because most people won't. It is a surefire way to make an incredible first impression. There are more reasons, but I'll cover those in a bit!

Face a light source

If you want your audience to connect to you, they need to see you properly. Daylight is easily the best light source, so face a window and invest in a ring light for when you have to present at night. Ensuring that the light is facing you rather than being above you will prevent creepy shadows from crossing your face.

DURING THE PRESENTATION

The goal is to transfer your energy through the screen so that your audience experiences the same emotional response that they would do if you were presenting in person. Everything we've covered in this section of the book applies, with a few little tweaks:

Connect with your voice

This will be a lot easier now you're not sitting down because your posture isn't restricting your vocal range.

Tweak: Add an extra second to the length of your pauses.

Connect with your body: use eye contact

Focus your gaze to the webcam or just below it. This will make your audience feel like you are talking directly to them. It's incredibly powerful when done well.

Tweak: By positioning your presentation notes and the audience's videos just below the webcam, your gaze will be naturally drawn towards it.

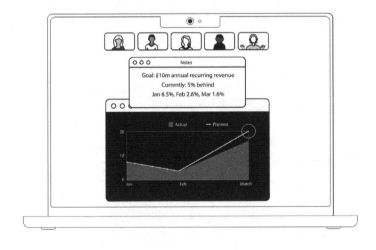

Connect with your body: use your hands

Gesturing as you would do normally will help to make sure you are as engaging online as you are in person.

Tweak: Have your hands a little higher than they would be normally so that they come into the camera frame occasionally.

Connect with your slides

We've already seen how using slides can make it harder for you to connect with your audience. This is particularly the case on video conferencing platforms that give slides the whole screen and shrink you to the size of a postage stamp.

Tweak: Instead of using a blank slide for the moments in your presentation where they aren't necessary, stop sharing them completely so that you take up the whole screen. It only takes a second to bring them back up when you need them. Aim to deliver at least half of your presentation without the deck.

These tweaks will take you from a forgettable 4 to at least a memorable 7. And while it might seem like a lot to take on, most of it will happen naturally, so long as you stand up.

TIP

——

A hack for hybrid presenting

Occasionally, you're going to find you've got to present to an in-person and online audience. Follow these steps and you'll be absolutely fine.

Welcome your online audience at the earliest opportunity. There's nothing worse than feeling like you've been forgotten about. So make a point of directing your gaze into the camera lens when you do.

Use names. In fact, this is worth doing in all online presentation scenarios. As an audience member, there's nothing like being mentioned publicly to keep you paying attention!

Address your in-person audience 95% of the time. In a perfect world, position the webcam among the rest of the audience, in which case you can treat it like everyone else.

Involve your online audience in any Q and A/discussion. A nice gesture might be to take questions from the online audience first.

Summary of Part 2

W
ith these tools, you have the potential to engage and influence your audience. You know how to give your words weight, make a lasting impression on your audience and use slides to enhance your message; both in person and online. With deliberate practice, each of these elements will come together to form your own unique style of presenting. When you can command the room, you'll be ready for the next section on learning how to read the room, tailor your delivery and build a rapport with your audience.

Until then, take one tool at a time and practise it deliberately.

CONNECT WITH YOUR VOICE

Pitch: Inflect down at the end of your sentences to show confidence in what you're saying.

Pace: Aim to start and finish 15% slower than your usual conversational speed. In the middle, vary the pace by speeding up for excitement, and slowing down for impact.

Power: Vary your volume to change the energy in the room. In the opening section of your talk, contrast your delivery style with the energy level of the room. In the closing section of your talk, ask yourself how you want your audience to feel. Soften your volume to create a calming, reassuring energy, and increase it to create a high-energy, exciting finish.

Pause: Use pauses to heighten the emotional experience. Aim to pause:

- before and after your first sentence

- after asking a question

- before and after every power statement.

CONNECT WITH YOUR BODY

Smile: Make it the first and last thing you do in your presentation.

Eye contact: Address every part of the room across your presentation. If you're speaking to a small group, aim to make eye contact with everyone.

Hands: Give them something to do. Keep your elbows by your side, with your hands just in front of you. Don't over-think it; let your hands tell their story.

CONNECT WITH YOUR PASSION

Ask yourself this question just before every presentation you deliver:

Why does this presentation matter to you?

Then channel that passion to get your message across.

CONNECT WITH YOUR SLIDES

Rule 1: Slides always come last. Ask yourself, what can slides say that I can't?

Rule 2: Use a blank slide when you don't need a visual aid. Aim for at least half of your presentation to be without slides.

Rule 3: The 1-second rule. If a slide isn't digestible in a second, it needs to be simplified. Stick to one message per slide.

Rule 4: Lead with your words, not with your slides. Give each slide a trigger word to ensure that your audience's curiosity is peaked when you reveal it.

CONNECT WITH YOUR AUDIENCE ONLINE

Before the presentation:

Stand up. Ensure the webcam is at eye height. Face a window/light source.

During the presentation:

Voice: Add an extra second to the length of your pauses.

Eye contact: Position your presentation notes/audience's videos just below your webcam.

Hands: Ensure your hands can be seen as part of your delivery.

Slides: Stop sharing your screen when there is no slide for your audience to see.

PART 3

CONFIDENCE

Confidence... it's not what you think it is

W hen I think back to my days running TEDx-Clapham, from the audience's perspective, every speaker would have been described as looking 'confident'.

But there is a lot more to confidence than what your audience can see. How a presenter might look and sound to an audience is often very different from how they might feel. Behind the scenes the tension was palpable, and the lengths some of the presenters would go to to create this façade of confidence might surprise you.

Some would hide in the nooks and crannies of the theatre rehearsing their scripts for the one hundredth time that day because they didn't trust themselves to remember their words. Others would be found trying to power-pose their way into a confident state or breathe themselves into a state of calm.

They were making me nervous on their behalf! None of them slipped up, but I worried about what might have happened if they did. It was like they were walking a tightrope: one mistake and their illusion would be shattered.

Looking back now, these were signs that I had more to learn. They revealed a gap in my expertise, both as a coach and as a presenter. I'd spent months working with them to craft messages that I would have been proud to deliver. I'd provided them with all sorts of tools to help them manage their nerves on the day so that they would *look* confident. But I'd spent no time helping them to *become* confident. The truth is, back then, I didn't know how to do this.

We all too often associate confidence with outer attributes: the way we carry ourselves, the words we use and the way we say them. The 'fake it till you make it' narrative that has plagued the internet in recent years results in a kind of confidence that is wafer thin.

We spend hours agonising over the message, attempting to commit those words to memory and psyching ourselves up, waiting for our turn. And when it comes, we cross our fingers and hope.

The result? A presentation that feels like a memory test.

The success of a presentation shouldn't be about making it through without forgetting your words or making a fool of yourself.

In this section of the book, I'm going to show you how to train your inner confidence so that you can bring presenting in high-stakes situations into your comfort zone. You're going to learn how to quieten the mind, overcome your nerves and how to keep things together when they don't go to plan.

Confidence is an internal state of trust. And it is a constant work in progress.

Do you present with the thinking brain or the doing brain?

———

There are two ways you can deliver a presentation: with your thinking brain or with your doing brain. Let me explain.

The thinking brain has a very calculated and controlled approach to presenting. Its primary goal is to do everything in its power to ensure you deliver the message you've prepared as accurately as possible. Then, if the presenter has had any exposure to communication training before, its secondary goal is to incorporate as much of that as possible into the delivery itself.

The result is a style of presentation that comes across as forced and unnatural. When you're using the thinking brain, it feels like you're presenting in a pressure cooker because it's in overdrive trying to get everything right.

In the best case, the presenter looks like they've spent too much time at Toastmasters. They've gone into 'presentation mode' and have a delivery that is so polished, it's almost robotic and inauthentic.

In the worst case, the thinking brain becomes so consumed with remembering everything perfectly that brain fog manifests and eventually the mind goes blank mid-presentation.

When the thinking brain is in control, you can only project outer confidence – the confidence that your audience can see.

The doing brain has a more uninhibited and fluid approach. Its goal is to keep your presentation's purpose and message front of mind but let the rest take care of itself. It knows that the presentation outline (the Speedy Speech-Writing Framework) can provide the necessary prompts you need to stay on track, so it is happy for each section to be delivered in the way that feels right in the moment itself.

The result is a style of presenting that comes across as conversational and relatable. When the doing brain is presenting, it feels effortless. The mind is quiet, and finding the right words is easy because there is no cognitive overload to disrupt your path.

The doing brain unlocks inner confidence – the type of confidence you can feel.

When you present with the doing brain for the first time, you will feel nothing short of unstoppable. And so you should. It is the realisation of a superpower, and when you're able to harness it, you will be able to handle any high-stakes presentation that is thrown at you.

From this point onwards, I would like you to actively differentiate between the two processes. You now have a 'thinking brain' and a 'doing brain'.

Now, to many of you reading this, the idea of presenting with the doing brain probably doesn't just sound like bliss, it sounds like the stuff of legend. Something to aspire to but not something you're likely to ever reach. This couldn't be further from the truth.

In fact, every single one of you is a proficient 'doing brain' communicator. You communicate with your doing brain every single day. In low-stakes environments, like when you're catching up with a friend, you don't think about what you're going to say or how you're going to say it, you just say it. So it's possible! Now it's about learning how to do it when you have planned what you're going to say and while you have a group of important people staring at you.

Both brains will play a part in making this happen.

Because of its perfectionist nature, your thinking brain is perfectly primed to help you prepare your presentation. It's going to help you get clear on your message, shape the audience journey and maybe even persuade you to practise your presentations a few times. But that is where its role ends.

To unlock inner confidence, all delivery responsibilities must be handed over to the doing brain. The problem is, the thinking brain finds it very difficult to relinquish control. It doesn't trust the doing brain to get the job done, despite the fact that the doing brain is far more skilled and experienced at communicating. For this to happen, you need to learn how to let go of the thinking brain.

Unlock confidence by learning to let go

LET GO OF YOUR WORDS

Give yourself permission to speak from the heart

Take a moment to consider this question:
On a scale of 1–10, how detailed do you like your notes to be for a typical presentation?

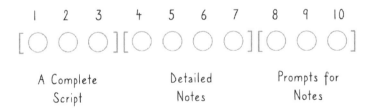

Your answer to this question could be an accurate reflection of your inner confidence levels in a presentation context.

I mentioned at the beginning of this chapter that confidence is an internal state of trust. Well, people who trust themselves do not need a complete script to stay on track. Not because they've spent countless hours memorising every word, but because they know their subject matter inside out and they back themselves to be able to deliver it effectively in the moment.

If you've been asked by senior leadership to present on a particular topic, it's because there is no one more qualified to do it than you. The likelihood is that what you've been asked to present is something you have been living and breathing for a significant period of time. If you were delivering the same content in a conversational setting, the idea of having everything written out beforehand would feel ridiculous!

Your score says a lot about your mindset as a presenter. It's not about whether you use your notes or how well you use them, it's an indication of how much you trust yourself in a high-pressure environment.

A score between 1–3 suggests you have low levels of inner confidence

Your script is your comfort blanket. It provides you and your thinking brain with a sense of control in what is a highly stressful situation. It might feel like having a script to fall back on gives you one less thing to worry about, but in reality:

• Preparing your presentations probably takes you hours longer than it should do because you get trapped in a level of detail that your audience won't remember anyway.

- Your thinking brain tempts you into reading the script even when you don't need to, and every time you do, you lose the connection you have with your audience.

- Your presentations still feel stressful because you're so consumed in what you're saying that you have no idea whether or not your message is landing.

I know this because I'm speaking from experience! Years of delivering workshops over video made me lazy. I got complacent (and really good at reading in a conversational way) and have had to rebuild my inner confidence by slowly weening myself off my scripts.

Letting go of your words – Stage 1

Make the transition from complete script to detailed notes.

A score between 4–7 suggests you have medium levels of inner confidence

Having detailed notes on hand ensures that you're not going to miss anything out. If you're at the lower end of this category, your notes consist of a mixture of mini-paragraphs and long-sentenced bullet points. It's a step in the right direction, but while your quest for accuracy might appease your thinking brain, your audience will feel like you care more about reeling off your list than you do about them.

You'll certainly be more conscious of your audience, but the mid-presentation stress will surface when you can't find your place in the depth of your notes.

At this level, there will be moments in your presentations where you find your flow and let your doing brain take the reins. Each time this happens is a sign your inner confidence is developing. This is something to be celebrated, then it's something to build on. Decrease the detail of your notes and you will increase the frequency of these moments.

Letting go of your words – Stage 2

Make the transition from paragraph chunks to bullet points. For example:

4. BACKGROUND

GOAL	CURRENTLY
£10m annual recurring revenues	5% behind Jan 6.5%, Feb 2.6%, Mar 1.6%

INSIGHT 1	INSIGHT 2
Bad review went viral	Customer Lifetime value drop

A score between 8–10 suggests you have high levels of inner confidence

To you, a full script or detailed notes feel like a constraint. That's why your presentation notes contain a mixture of key words that serve as prompts along with the odd power sentence here and there that you need to nail. This set-up gives you peace of mind because:

• Preparing for your presentations doesn't take up a disproportionate amount of your time, which means you resent having to do them less.

• Without a script to tempt you with, the thinking brain has no choice but to allow the doing brain to take care of delivery responsibilities.

• The prompts ensure you stay on track, while giving you the flexibility to deliver them in a way that feels most appropriate for the moment you find yourself in.

By keeping your notes light, you are creating the perfect environment for your doing brain to flourish. Each time you step up to present with prompts you are making a statement of intent to yourself – that you've got this. You are starting your presentations from a position of strength.

Letting go of your words – Stage 3

Make the transition from detailed bullets to prompts. For example:

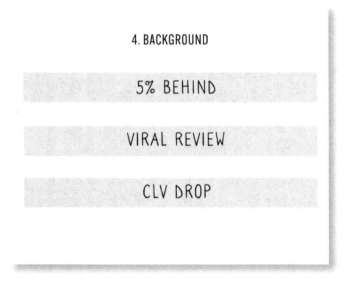

4. BACKGROUND

5% BEHIND

VIRAL REVIEW

CLV DROP

No doubt you may already be experiencing resistance at the idea of delivering your next presentation with prompts like these for presenter notes. Wherever you are on the journey from complete script to prompts, taking the next step always requires a leap of faith. Remember, this is a journey that you can embark on at your own pace. The steepness of your learning curve is a decision that is completely in your control.

HOW TO FAST-TRACK YOUR INNER CONFIDENCE

If you'd prefer to rip off the Band-Aid rather than drag the process out, here is how to do it:

Step 1: Create a prompt-only version of your presentation

Or cheat like me and use the presentation outline you've already created with the Speedy Speech-Writing Framework. Print out the sheet, cut each section out, and you have your cue cards ready to go!

Step 2: Practise with prompts

Use the time you would have spent writing out your script to practise your presentation out loud using only prompts. Take one section at a time and rehearse, refine, repeat. When you're happy with the general flow, you can start connecting sections together.

It will come out slightly differently every time and that's ok – in fact, that's the point! You're not trying to repeat it so it comes out 'perfectly' every time. You'll know when you're on the right track when it takes you less time to communicate each section. Not because you're speaking any faster, but because the flow has become familiar. (This is where MicDrop Analytics comes into its own as a presenting tool, because you can use it to measure your improvement.)

Step 3: Create your final presenter notes (if applicable)

An effective time to do this is the morning of your presentation. You might feel like the prompts you've been practising with are enough, in which case you can skip this step completely (hello, high inner confidence!). If not, feel free to pad out your prompts with anything extra you need, safe in the knowledge that you are already going into the presentation with far more confidence (and far less detailed notes) than you would have done if you hadn't completed this exercise.

What happens when we ditch the thinking brain

On one of my coaching programmes, I'd given the cohort a week to prepare a three-minute presentation to deliver to the group. Cue Catherine, a finance director at an ecommerce company who wanted to bring delivering updates to the board into her comfort zone. She delivers her presentation to the group, and before I have a chance to ask her how she found it, she tells the group how awfully she thought it went. To be fair, it wasn't her best. When I asked her why, she put it down to not spending enough time preparing the message.

A surprising observation given she'd read the whole thing out from start to finish. Catherine's thinking brain was in complete control and it was consumed with accuracy. You can almost hear her thinking brain saying to her doing brain, 'Look, just leave the presenting to me!'

Thirty minutes later, I was doing a storytelling exercise with the group. I brought Catherine on, conversed with her for a bit and asked her about something that had happened in the last quarter at work. She proceeded to speak for the next three minutes uninterrupted and completely off the cuff in front of the whole group. No script in sight. The story she told wouldn't have looked out of place in a boardroom. It was meaningful, engaging and memorable. For the very first time in her career, she had allowed her doing brain to take control of the presenting.

So what actually happened here? By initially disguising the exercise as a conversation, we tricked the thinking brain into believing it wasn't needed. Now, instead of creating a full script, Catherine simply practises her presentations with prompts. That leap of faith has unlocked an inner confidence that she never knew existed.

LET GO OF YOUR EXPECTATIONS (AND THEIRS)

Handle pressure like an olympian

There are a lot of similarities between athletes and presenters. For starters, the time spent preparing to perform is disproportionately long compared to the amount of time you spend *actually* performing. Add to that the fact that there is an expectation to perform to a high standard and then, to top it all off, you've only got one opportunity to make it count. It's no wonder that we 'feel the pressure'.

Pressure comes from expectation:

- The expectation that our audience has for us to deliver the presentation. (External)

- The expectation we place on ourselves to deliver the presentation. (Internal)

As the days tick down to the presentation, the expectation ramps up. This is called expectation inflation. Learn to overcome it and presentations that feel out of your depth will move into your comfort zone.

External expectation inflation

Presenting to people you need to impress can be very intimidating. We're all guilty of building our audience up to be far scarier than they really are. We fall into the trap of giving too much weight to their seniority, or struggle with the fact that there are people in the room who have more experience or knowledge about the presentation topic.

This can be all-consuming. When we let external expectation get the better of us, we trick ourselves into thinking that our presentation is the first, last and only thing our audience thinks about each day.

On paper this sounds ridiculous, but it feels so real when you're caught up in it.

The truth is that your audience will not have given your presentation a second thought until you start speaking. They're far more concerned about what's going on in their own lives. The CEO you're presenting to this afternoon may be intimidatingly impressive, but they're also human. They too spill ketchup on their shirt at lunch or look like an idiot tripping on a kerb on the way to work.

There is often a huge disparity between what we think our audience is expecting of us and what they are actually expecting. They're not expecting a TED talk, they're expecting a 6/10. That is the score the leaders I interviewed gave the average presentation at work. One leader even remarked that 'to expect 7/10s would leave me continually disappointed!'

Suddenly, delivering an insightful and memorable presentation doesn't feel so unachievable…

Internal expectation inflation

Internal expectation comes from the fact that you're a high achiever and set yourself very high standards. Let me tell you who else sets themselves high standards.

Olympians.

I've been lucky enough to work with a few. They've won medals too, so they know a thing or two about how to perform at their peak when it matters the most.

All of them shift their mindset when they switch from training to competition. In training, they do everything in their power to achieve their full potential and a 10/10 performance. But in competition, they expect nothing. They let go of it all. This is because they realise that:

- to perform at their best, they need to be relaxed

- expecting a 10/10 performance in competition is setting themselves up to fail. There are all sorts of factors they have no control over that would need to work in their favour.

As a presenter, you would do well to adopt a similar approach. So treat yourself like an athlete. Train for a 10/10 presentation by:

- having the courage to get clarity on the presentation ask

- pinpointing your purpose and message

- creating an outline that takes your audience on a journey

- practising with prompts

and finally...

- rehearsing your presentation in front of a real human (ideally a colleague whose opinion you respect and who will tell you exactly as it is). Athletes make their training environments as real as possible, and so should you.

To maximise this opportunity, here are some questions you can ask them afterwards to ensure you get the exact feedback you need:

1. **What was your main takeaway?**

   This question will highlight the strength of your message. Does their answer match up with yours? If not, why not?

2. **Where did you switch off?**

   A great question to highlight the sections in your talk where your delivery got lax, your content is dry, or both!

3. **What is your counterargument?**

   This will help you to highlight any holes/weaknesses in your narrative.

When you've done all the presentation prep you can, it's time to deflate your expectations for the performance itself. To do this requires a mindset shift.

Training for a 10/10 can be a useful mindset to help you prepare, but if it's allowed to continue into the performance it will be debilitating. Rather than working towards the best possible outcome, a kinder approach is to opt for a 'good enough' outcome.

To deflate your expectations, ask yourself:

What is a good enough presentation?

For me, it's a 6/10.

A 6/10 will still get your message across and will still be worth your audience's time. There's still room for the odd mistake or unexpected interruption, and you'll be in a far better position to handle them because you're more relaxed.

A 6/10 feels far more achievable and far less overwhelming than aiming for a 10/10. But most importantly of all, the mindset will unlock the chance of hitting a 7/10, or even an 8/10 or 9/10.

This isn't about setting low standards; it's about creating the mindset for high performance.

LET GO OF YOUR JUDGEMENT

Build shatter-proof inner confidence

Judgement is the act of attaching a positive or negative opinion to something that's happened. When we're presenting we do this a lot!

Imagine you're up next to present, and you notice your heart is beating faster, your face feels flushed and your hands have got the shakes.

Negative judgement: Uh oh, I'm nervous. **Nerves are bad.** I perform badly when I'm nervous.

Or…

Positive judgement: Ooh, I must be nervous! **Nerves are good.** They help me get into the zone.

Maybe you're mid-presentation. You notice that most of the audience is typing away on their laptops.

Negative judgement: **This presentation is going terribly.** No one is paying attention!

Or…

Positive judgement: **This presentation is going well.** Everyone's taking notes!

At first glance, it might seem like one attitude makes you a more confident presenter and one doesn't, but actually, neither judgement is helpful.

One makes your confidence plummet, while the other lures you into a false sense of security. Attaching a value to everything you're experiencing forces you to think about your relationship with presenting in a very binary way. It becomes an all-or-nothing affair. It's why the stakes always seem so high; there is no middle ground.

Throughout a presentation, these micro-judgements build. They increase the pressure, make us tense up and cause us to lose confidence in our message. Then, when the presentation's done, it culminates in the most destructive judgement of all: either it went well, or it didn't.

It's easy to see how lots of 'didn't go well's become a self-fulfilling prophecy. And you'd be forgiven for thinking that lots of 'did go well's would result in building your confidence. But you'd be wrong.

Imagine you're on a roll, building on a streak of presentations that have 'gone well'. Your confidence begins to increase. Finally, you've turned a corner in your presentation journey! And then, out of nowhere, you have a shocker. Your confidence drops like a house of cards and you feel like you are back to square one (even though you're not).

'You're only as good as your last...' has got to be one of the most toxic narratives in the world of high-pressure performance. It encourages what I call momentum-based confidence.

'I nailed that last presentation. I can't let my standard slip now.'

This kind of attitude inflates internal expectation. The longer the streak continues, the more nervous you'll be ahead of your next presentation.

Both positive and negative judgements have a detrimental effect on confidence. They result in a presenter who is at the mercy of what's going on around them to dictate how confident they feel.

But inner confidence that is built on faith rather than past results is shatter-proof.

The way to stop judgement is to practise observation. Observing is noticing the blank expression on the faces of your audience members and holding back from giving it a label. It is having an awareness of your mouth going dry without associating it with something good or bad. Instead, approach what you notice with a sense of curiosity, rather than drawing a conclusion from it.

Observation without judgement is the key to quietening the mind, and over time it will help you to build an unshakeable inner confidence.

LET GO OF YOUR NERVES

Reframe the sensations to work with them

There isn't one person on this planet that doesn't have to deal with nerves, anxiety and stage-fright ahead of delivering a presentation that really matters. So before we start, let's make one thing very clear:

Confident people get nervous too.

Nerves are what surface when our fight or flight response is triggered. A series of biochemical changes occur in the body that result in a racing pulse, an increase in blood pressure, shortness of breath, sweaty palms, a dry mouth, shaky hands, a wobbly voice and, of course, butterflies in our tummies.

Science says that the fight or flight response is designed to keep us safe, though I'm not sure how useful sweaty hands are in a life or death situation. But in the context of a presentation, if not managed correctly, it results in us suffering from self-doubt, feeling very awkward and generally despising the whole presentation experience.

Ironically, many adopt a fight or flight strategy when it comes to managing nerves. They 'fight' by trying to suppress them in some way (often by attempting to think themselves out of them), or take 'flight' by trying to ignore them completely. Both approaches are energy-sapping and ineffective. This happens because they've made the mistake of judging the feelings they're experiencing.

Nerves are neither good or bad. They just are.

So since they're there, what can we do to work with them rather than against them?

Reframe the sensations

Biochemically, there is very little difference between nerves and excitement. If you can use these sensations as an energetic asset, it can make all the difference. A certain level of nervousness or stress can actually lead to a better performance:

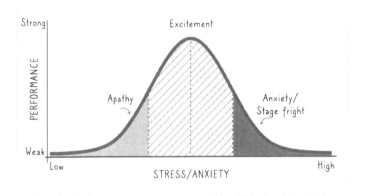

The bottom line is this: without your fight or flight response, you will not achieve peak performance, so rather than try to fight it, learn to embrace it.

Schedule your nerves

If your nerves are going to come anyway, you might as well find a time for them that suits you. Better that than allowing them to build up from the moment you find out you've got a presentation to deliver.

When nerves have time to take hold, they are much harder to manage. So schedule some time in your diary for them. Doing so creates psychological boundaries. If you feel your nerves surfacing before you're ready, remind yourself that you have allotted time for these feelings later on and make a point of cracking on with something else to distract you. In terms of scheduling in the nerves, I've found the day before a presentation to be the sweet spot. Close enough to feel real and with a night's sleep in place to create a reset.

I find this technique incredibly liberating. I still experience nerves before delivering a workshop or presentation (something which was once a real source of shame given my job), but since I started scheduling them, they've never showed up to quite the same extent.

Develop a pre-presentation ritual

Inspired by the coping mechanisms that athletes have to enable them to perform under pressure, I created a pre-presentation ritual to help me turn nerves into excitement. It's proved to be a game-changer, especially because (alongside any physical symptoms) my nerves tend to manifest in an unhealthy amount of negative self-talk.

I'm sharing it in the hope that you'll steal it and tweak it.

Conscious of the benefits of a good night's sleep, my ritual begins the evening before. I do a complete run-through of the presentation just before bed, using a mixture of Mic-Drop Analytics and my wife to keep me accountable. You might think that focusing on the presentation just before going to bed is a recipe for a sleepless night, and it'd be better to distract myself from it completely. But I find that if I've put in the work before getting into bed, it gives my brain closure. It's one less thing to think about while I sleep.

When I wake up the next day, it's time to address my fight or flight response.

My theory is simple. If my body wants to fight or take flight, then I'm going to give it exactly what it wants. So I go for a run. It gets me out of the house, away from my laptop and prompts, and rebalances my biochemistry by using up excess adrenaline and lowering my cortisol (stress hormone) levels.

On the run, I do three things:

- Smile at people I run past. Some of them smile back! And it's a timely reminder that my audience probably isn't going to be as scary as I've built them up to be.

- Visualise all of the negative self-talk being expelled from my body with each exhale.

- Listen to some music. The music I choose depends on my mood. If I feel as though I'm going into my shell, I'll listen to something that's going to bring me back out. A bit of prog house does the job nicely. If I'm feeling pumped up and I need to calm down, then perhaps something classical. But more often than not, I take myself way too seriously, so I resort to 70s and 80s feel-good hits: ABBA, Queen and Chic... I literally have a party in my ears!

When I arrive home, I open my front door, step into my house and say, 'It's game time.' No negativity is allowed from this point forwards. It's time to let go of my words, expectations and judgements. I remind myself to just see what happens, and what will be will be.

TIP

▬

Shift your mindset with music

Music is the fastest way to shift your mindset. If and when you're short of time, or the effects of your pre-presentation ritual have worn off, one song has the power to take you out of your head and into your body (from the thinking to the doing brain).

Find your own 'game song'. A song that makes you feel great, gives you energy and helps you channel your passion. Then get into the habit of listening to it as close to the time of your presentation as possible.

To give you a head start, I've created a playlist of songs designed to get you out of your head and into the zone ahead of an important presentation.

See Tool 13 in the Toolkit.

EXERCISE

Develop your courage with
the commitment calendar

Speaking in front of an audience regularly will dramatically improve your ability to work with your nerves. It's called exposure therapy. The more regularly your fight or flight response is triggered, the better your body and your mind become at managing it.

If you only present when you have to, your development as a presenter is at the mercy of others. You're a reactive presenter. This means that if you're only asked to present once a quarter, or even once a month, by the time the next one comes around your body has forgotten everything that it learned the last time round. In other words, you're lacking match practice.

You need to become a proactive presenter if you really want to bring public speaking into your comfort zone. This means actively finding opportunities to trigger your fight or flight response by speaking in intimidating environments. You can do this by speaking up in a meeting full of senior people when you'd normally keep quiet, giving a toast at a dinner party, or volunteering a question at a conference or work event.

These moments may seem small, but they are mighty. Each one is a courageous act of inner confidence. My challenge to you is to make exposure therapy a habit by speaking up once a week for a year. Set yourself the challenge of triggering your fight or flight response once a week and use the commitment calendar to help (Tool 14 in the Toolkit).

COMMITMENT CALENDAR

"We are what we repeatedly do.
Excellence, then, is not an act, but a habit."

- ARISTOTLE

The purpose of the commitment calendar is to make speaking up a habit. There are 52 circles, one for each week of the year, and your job is to find one opportunity to speak per week. Then celebrate taking it by ticking off a circle.

Here are the rules:

1. Situations where you've been asked to speak don't count. Inner confidence doesn't come from others telling you to do something; it comes from making the decision yourself.

2. You can fall behind and catch up, but you can't get ahead. If you are on track (e.g. you're 18 weeks in and have 18 ticked circles), you can't tick any more circles until the following week. However, if there were no opportunities one week and you fall behind, if you find yourself with several opportunities the next week, you can use those to catch up. This helps to mitigate the fact that you might have three chances one week, and none the next.

What to do when things go wrong mid-presentation

few years back I was invited to deliver a PechaKucha presentation. It's a format where you present
20 slides for 20 seconds each, with a timer con-
trolling the slides. Labour a point for too long and everyone will know because the slides won't wait! They're great
fun – if you're not delivering one!

The invitation to take part came about after having
recently become a member of this exclusive community of
entrepreneurs. The calibre of the members is intimidatingly
high. No doubt you'd recognise the names of some of the
companies my audience were responsible for founding. The
problem (aside from the fact I couldn't exactly say no to

the invitation) was that my reputation had preceded me. I'd worked with a few people in the community and they'd very kindly sung my praises publicly to the group.

To say expectation inflation was getting the better of me was an understatement. If I got this wrong then I'd forever be known among these high rollers as the public speaking coach that can't speak in public.

Luckily, I'd come up with a masterplan... or so I thought. I was going to pretend I'd forgotten my words for the first 20 seconds, and then have 'Gotcha' come up as the second slide. A stupidly high-risk strategy that resulted in me spending the next three weeks dreading the thing.

Fast forward to the big day and I'm introduced onto the stage as 'the public speaking coach who's worked with entrepreneurial legends!'

The applause softens and I hear one of the founders chip in, 'No pressure!'

Just as I'm about to start, I notice the technician skip the first slide and proceed straight to the 'Gotcha' slide. My masterplan had been foiled and the joke my whole presentation had been pinned on was ruined.

Two seconds of panic later, the slides cut out completely.

I was left standing up in front of some of the country's most impressive entrepreneurs with no plan and nowhere to hide.

So, what's the worst thing that you can imagine happening to you while you're presenting?!

It might seem like a counterintuitive question, but it's one I often ask in my workshops.

You'd be forgiven for thinking that asking such a question would do more damage than good. We are taught that focusing on the 'negatives' is self-defeating or pessimistic, but actually, choosing to confront the things that could go wrong is both courageous and smart.

Some of the answers I get back include: what if my mind goes blank? What if the tech stops working? What if I get asked a question that I don't know the answer to?

While these are things we think will be a complete nightmare if they happen, the reality is that the people you're talking to won't be bothered if you handle them well, regardless of how senior they are.

Stepping up to present knowing you've got a back-up plan in place if the unexpected happens is going to take your confidence to new heights.

So here are the five most common challenges you are likely to face mid-presentation, along with a fail-safe way of handling them every time. Bookmark this section and read through it the night before your next presentation so you've got them in mind.

YOUR PRESENTATION DISASTER RECOVERY PLAN

1. What to do if your mind goes blank

Forgetting your words is a matter of when, not if. Learning to accept that removes the pressure to get everything right and unlocks a new level of inner confidence.

Step 1: Don't make it awkward. Don't apologise. Instead, tell the audience!

> *'I have completely forgotten where I was going with that! Let me check my notes... Ah! That's right...'*

Step 2: Carry on as though it never happened. Watching someone forget their words is as uncomfortable for the audience as it is for the presenter. If it's not a big deal for you, it doesn't become one for them.

2. What to do if your tech fails

This is also a case of when, not if. The 'when' being when you least expect it/at your presentation's most important point/ when you are most in your flow (delete as appropriate!).

Step 1: Pre-empt by thinking SNAP.

- Slides: Have you run through them on the computer you're using for the presentation itself?

- Notifications: Are they turned off or will everyone be able to read the text you get from your partner halfway through?

- Audio: Do you need to turn your volume up or share your sound?

- Power: Do you need to connect to a power source?

Step 2: Notice it (without judgement) and acknowledge it to break the tension in the room.

'Ahh, perfect timing!'

Step 3: Tell your audience the plan. For anything under 30 seconds:

'Don't worry, that's a quick fix...'

Then go fix it!

For anything longer:

'That looks fun... Don't worry, we can carry on without, I'll send you the slides later.'

Then shut the laptop and carry on.

Notice there's no apology. This is because it is (probably) not your fault, and from a psychological standpoint apologising might do your confidence for the rest of the presentation more harm than good.

Remember, your audience will only tense up if you do. When the unexpected happens, the only thing they'll be thinking about is how pleased they are it's happened to you rather than them! So you can overcome this challenge, safe in the knowledge that everyone will still be on your side.

3. What to do if you get asked a question you don't know the answer to

It might feel like one, but it's not a test. The questioner isn't trying to catch you out. They're curious, which is proof that your presentation was engaging!

Step 1: Take a moment to think about what you've been asked. Remember the power of the pause – you don't have to rush headlong into trying to answer.

'That's a good question...'

Step 2: Own your 'ignorance'!

'The honest answer is I don't know. But I will get back to you with an answer by the end of the day. Does anyone else have any thoughts on this?'

We can spot bullshit a mile off. Blagging your way through an answer in an attempt to save face will not fool anyone.

Honesty shows confidence and audiences are far more likely to respect, remember and trust those who show it.

By opening the question up to the audience, it enables the conversation to continue without any awkwardness.

4. What to do if someone challenges your point mid-presentation

A challenge can feel like a personal attack, especially if they're interrupting you to do it. If not handled well, it can derail your presentation.

Step 1: Turn the attention back on the heckler (while buying yourself some time).

Smile 'I didn't catch that, could you say that again?'

Step 2: Clarify what you've heard.

'Ah, so you're saying that…'

By creating some buffer between the initial challenge and your response, it will allow you to approach the challenge from a place of curiosity rather than a place of defence, diffusing any tension as a result. Then following up with a clarifying statement turns a potential confrontation into a collaborative conversation by establishing a common understanding. At this point, the best path forward will be much clearer.

5. What to do if you're presenting remotely with dodgy Wi-Fi

Hopefully it's because you're somewhere exotic… Managing dodgy Wi-Fi requires a different approach to tech failure.

Step 1: Be upfront.

> *'Hi everyone. Just to forewarn you, my internet is playing up! If we start to experience any problems, it's more likely to be me than it is you, so do let me know if I start cutting out.'*

Step 2: Share the plan.

> *'If it becomes an issue, I'll turn off my video to preserve bandwidth. I've assigned Will as a co-host, just in case I lose connection. That way everyone will stay in the meeting and I will reconnect as soon as I can.'*

Mentioning issues at the beginning prevents everyone getting defensive about the quality of their own connection. Now they're aware of it, they're far less likely to be frustrated by it, especially when you've shared the plan.

For bonus points you can always give the person you are assigning as co-host a heads up prior to the meeting, and give them something they can do if you get disconnected. For example, discuss a relevant topic or put the audience into break-outs if you were already planning to give them an exercise.

The secret to handling all unexpected incidents is to make them as forgettable as possible.

When I found myself standing in front of all those entrepreneurs at the beginning of my PechaKucha presentation, that's exactly what I did. Instead of standing on stage waiting awkwardly for the tech to be fixed, I said:

'I'm not going to lie, that is such a relief! I honestly don't know how I convinced myself that this was a good idea, but the plan was to spend the first 20 seconds pretending I'd forgotten my words. If you thought this was an awkward start, that would have been much worse: I can't act! I've been saved by the tech!'

My confession was met with warm smiles, laughter and general positivity. The audience couldn't have been more supportive. I relaxed and the sound of audience chatter filled the void while the tech was fixed. My PechaKucha (minus the opener) went to plan. And though I got lots of positive comments about it, not one person mentioned the disaster itself. Which is exactly how it should be: completely unmemorable.

Summary of Part 3

A lot of what we've covered in this chapter is about learning how to let go. It's a habit that takes practice, and the changes are often unnoticeable and small, but by following this process your confidence will build and it will be unshakeable. The uncomfortable will become comfortable. You might even begin to enjoy the challenge. If and when you do, it's time to raise the stakes once again – whether it's delivering something department- or company-wide, speaking at an external conference, or maybe even stepping onto a thought leadership stage.

Until then, remember that confidence is a constant work in progress. So try to enjoy the journey.

Confidence is an internal state of trust and falls into two categories: outer confidence, the confidence that people see, and inner confidence, the confidence that you can feel. Inner confidence can only be achieved by learning how to hand over the presentation responsibilities from the thinking brain to the doing brain.

In order to do this you must:

LET GO OF EXPECTATION

Next time you've got a presentation to deliver, ask yourself:

What does good enough look like?

And then give it a score out of 10. If the answer is above a 7, you're putting unnecessary pressure on yourself.

LET GO OF JUDGEMENT

Judgement is the act of assigning a positive or negative value to everything that is happening while you present. It is the fastest way to overthink and make your confidence plummet.

Instead, practise the art of observation. Notice what's going on, without judgement. It will help you to stay present, your mind to stay clear, and your doing brain to react to what it sees accordingly, without the thinking brain wanting to step in and take over.

WORK WITH YOUR FIGHT OR FLIGHT RESPONSE, NOT AGAINST IT

Your fight or flight response is going to be triggered, and that's ok. Here are some ways to use it, so that you can reach a state of peak performance:

- There is a fine line between nerves and excitement. Can you reframe your nerves as excitement?

- Plan when you are going to allow any nerves (or excitement) to surface.

- Often the best ways to create shifts in your mind are through your body. Can you use exercise, music or breathing exercises to your advantage?

PLAN FOR MID-PRESENTATION DISASTER

Go through your disaster recovery plan the night before your presentation and remind yourself of exactly what you're going to do if the unexpected occurs. Whatever happens, the goal is simple: to make any 'disasters' as forgettable as possible.

As a general rule of thumb:

Step 1: Buy yourself some time by verbally acknowledging the event.

Step 2: Be clear with your audience about what is going to happen next.

CONCLUSION

___

A KINDER WAY TO MEASURE THE IMPACT OF YOUR PRESENTATIONS

One of the things you might have realised is that clarity, connection and confidence represent more than just the main sections of the book. They provide a means of measuring the three pillars of a presentation. Clarity is about your message, connection is about your audience and confidence is about you, the speaker.

Thinking about your presentations in this way gives you a simple, non-judgemental way of measuring your progress. After every presentation you deliver, ask yourself:

- Was my message clear?

- Was my audience connected?

- Did I feel confident?

It's a simple, useful and objective way of getting regular feedback on how you are progressing. Answering each question with yes/no is a great start, or you could measure each one on a scale of 1–10.

Your answers will help guide you in the direction of the area you might want to focus on in the next presentation you deliver. At which point you can revisit the corresponding section of the book, pick something to practise deliberately and incorporate it into your upcoming presentations.

They will be more memorable as a result. And you will impress the people that matter the most.

We've covered a lot in this book, though it probably won't be until you deliver your next presentation that you'll realise how far you've already come. You have all the tools you need to:

- deliver presentations that update, educate or persuade

- structure presentations with impact, while taking your audience on the journey they need to go on to ensure your message lands

- speak with gravitas and use your body language to change the energy in the room

- incorporate slides in a way that enhances your message rather than distracts your audience

- manage your nerves and quieten your mind

- build the type of confidence that doesn't plummet if a presentation fails to go your way.

Now it's time to put them to good use so that you can reap the benefits. When you do, I'd love to hear about it. I wrote this book because I think it can make a difference (and as you know, I thrive on outcomes). Normally, I get to see the progress my clients make directly, but unless you tell me, I'll never know, so do get in touch. My email is alex@alexmerry.com.

Some of you reading this might be wondering where you can go to get the exposure therapy you need and practise the skills you've learned in this book. If this is you, apply to become a member of my public speaking club, MicDrop. It's a place to:

- hone your speaking skills by practising regularly, in front of others, in a supportive environment

- build on the skills you've learned in this book with my on-demand training library

- get full access to my analytics platform so you can track and measure your progress

- find out about in-person speaking opportunities that you can use to build your professional brand.

There is a link to the application form in the Toolkit.

I also run workshops and programmes for teams. If you'd like to learn more, go to www.alexmerry.com.

With all the books that are out there in the world these days, there's no way this one is going to cut through the noise without some help from you. So if you have found this book useful, please post an Amazon/Google review, talk about it on social media and recommend it to friends and colleagues. It would make all the difference.

Thank you.